ALLERGIES,
Away!

ALLERGIES, Away!

Creative Eats and Mouthwatering Treats for Kids Allergic to Nuts, Dairy, and Eggs

Ginger Park and Frances Park

THOMAS DUNNE BOOKS

St. Martin's Griffin ∼ New York

THOMAS DUNNE BOOKS.
An imprint of St. Martin's Press.

www.thomasdunnebooks.com
www.stmartins.com

Design by Maura Fadden Rosenthal/MSpace

Library of Congress Cataloging-in-Publication Data

Park, Ginger
    Allergies, away! : creative eats and mouthwatering treats for kids allergic to nuts, dairy, and eggs / Ginger Park and Frances Park.—First edition.
        p. cm.
    Includes index.
    ISBN 978-1-250-00302-7 (trade paperback.)
    ISBN 978-1-250-03030-6 (e-book)
    1. Food allergy in children—Diet therapy—Recipes.   2. Food allergy—Diet therapy—Recipes.   I. Park, Frances.   II. Title.

    RJ386.5.P37 2013
    641.5'6318—dc23

                                        2013003257

St. Martin's Griffin books may be purchased for educational, business, or promotional use. For information on bulk purchases, please contact Macmillan Corporate and Premium Sales Department at 1-800-221-7945 extension 5442 or write special markets@macmillan.com.

First Edition: May 2013

10 9 8 7 6 5 4 3 2 1

DISCLAIMER

Because individuals' sensitivities to foods that trigger allergic reactions will vary greatly, readers should consult their physician or health-care professional about food choices. Individual readers are solely responsible for their own health-care decisions, and the authors and the publisher do not accept responsibility for any adverse effects individuals may claim to experience, whether directly or indirectly, based on information contained herein.

To Justin,
and to all children with food allergies

CONTENTS

ACKNOWLEDGMENTS

We're indebted to our agent, Mollie Glick, who believed in this project from the moment we shared stories about Justin and his food allergies with her. A huge hug of appreciation to Kat Brzozowski, our editor, whose enthusiasm and suggestions for the cookbook proved invaluable. Many thanks also to Leah Stewart, our copyeditor, for her keen eye.

We'd also like to acknowledge all the Web site advocating for educating people about food allergies. We wish we could name them all for creating a global platform for food allergy awareness that has given parents of allergic children comfort and hope. Among our favorite Web sites: www.Foodallergyliving.org, www.Foodallergy.org, www.Kidswithfoodallergies.org, and www.Faiusa.org (Food Allergy Initiative).

We're very grateful to Justin's family of aunts, uncles, cousins, and friends who encouraged us to write our book simply by loving our food. Special thanks to our mom and Justin's dad, who helped us out in the test kitchen. Our nature is to add a little bit of this, a little bit of that. The scientists in us were guided by their taste buds.

Last, we would like to thank our food-critic-in-residence, Justin. Not only for his five-star reviews, but for being the heartbeat of our family. We love you.

PREFACE

*A*llergies, Away! *Creative Eats and Mouth-watering Treats for Kids Allergic to Nuts, Dairy, and Eggs* features recipes and anecdotes for children who suffer from these most common food allergies. Unlike food intolerances, a true food allergy can be life-threatening and means that every crumb that touches your child's lips must be monitored and controlled. Restaurant dining, much less food from the cafeteria or movie popcorn, is out of the question. Halloween? Forget about it.

As the mom and aunt of a severely allergic child, we fretted not just about what to feed Justin but the social distress he might encounter as he reached school age. Suddenly, there'd be snack time to contend with, not to mention lunch hour and birthday parties. Feeling deprived is never fun, and picturing his sad face broke our hearts. On the flip side, it was also a great motivator.

The mission of *Allergies, Away!* is to provide a sunny,

hands-on approach to a serious condition by presenting a well-balanced menu of snacks, meals, and desserts for young allergy-sufferers that are so inviting they'll get in on the kitchen act. In the hopes of guiding parents and children on their own allergy journeys, we've provided "Allergy Reports," a timeline of Justin's medical allergy testing from age one to fourteen. From personal experience, we know how the journey can leave you feeling lost in the dark, so perhaps our reports will shed a little light on what can be a frustrating process. Our "Allergy Reports," however, are not meant to replace your own doctor's opinion of your child's condition.

As co-authors of many award-winning children's books, we write straight from the heart. Justin was the inspiration for *Allergies, Away!,* and for him we would comb the globe to find wholesome substitute ingredients for the foods he couldn't eat. Fortunately, with the help of natural food stores, imagination, and experimentation, our Hot and Bubbly Lasagna is so chewy and delicious, it might even wow Chef Mario Batali or Giada De Laurentiis. More important, our lasagna wows Justin, and we know it will wow your kid as well!

In the kitchen, with flour and sugar flying everywhere, the three of us can't help but have a ball. Mom Ginger serves as master chef, Francie is aunt slash sous chef, while Justin is our young food critic, rating everything we bake, steam, and fry on a one- to five-star scale. Only the five-star recipes have made the cut into this book.

Please note: We're neither doctors nor chefs. We're a mom and an aunt who love cooking for a child with allergies. Our hearts go into every pot, and so will yours.

ALLERGIES,
Away!

INTRODUCTION

*I*magine this: You're a kid in a chocolate shop watching everyone picking this one, that one, two of these, please, to their heart's content—everyone but you. Now imagine that your mom and aunt own the chocolate shop. Growing up, Ginger's son Justin never had the pleasure of enjoying a single treat from our shop, Chocolate Chocolate, in downtown Washington, DC. What we took for granted—absently nibbling on a Dark Chocolate–Dipped Caramel or gobbling a few Milk Hazelnut Pralines, the chew-crunch-velvety experience of rich chocolate—he absolutely couldn't. One second of abandon could cost him his life. The reason: Like more and more children today, he suffers from food allergies. Dr. Clifford W. Bassett, Medical Director of Allergy & Asthma Care of New York, says of the rise of pediatric food allergies, "It's a mini epidemic for sure."

How did this mini epidemic happen? No one can explain it, not even experts. Unfortunately, when it comes to food allergies, there are more questions than answers.

During Ginger's pregnancy, she gave up her fair share of vices. Lattes and Brie cheese? No sweat. Appletinis? No problem. Chocolate? Well, that was a bit more challenging. After all—just like her big sis Francie—she was born a chocoholic.

In the 1990s, pregnant women were advised to avoid chocolate, mostly due to the caffeine. The medical community has since changed their tune, but, back then, Ginger was doing everything she could to ensure a healthy baby. Now, trust us, there's nothing dainty about chocolate withdrawal when you're in a sweet boutique all day with gourmet chocolate truffles, pralines, and candy bars in your face. The daily temptation to dig into a bittersweet truffle had Ginger on her knees, salivating. If she wasn't making them, she was swooning over them. But one constant reminder kept her disciplined: her changing body.

Customers were always quipping:

"The first word out of his mouth will be 'chocolate!'" "Your baby's going to be the luckiest kid on earth, having a mom who owns a chocolate shop!" "Better watch him or he'll eat all the profits!"

Ginger enjoyed a healthy pregnancy, playing tennis through her sixth month and jogging on the treadmill until the day before she gave birth. Her hearty appetite never waned as she feasted on fruits and vegetables, and, of course, loaded up on foods rich in folic acid and calcium. Basically, she did everything humanly possible to give birth to a healthy child.

Justin's birth was quick and uncomplicated. On the morning of April 14, 1998, while waiting on a customer at our shop, she went into labor. She was still packing up bonbons between contractions for customers until her unborn child nearly knocked her off her feet—it was time to go to the hospital! She and hubby Skip checked in at five o'clock that afternoon; by nine o'clock that night, she was holding a precious seven-pound baby boy.

"Justin Young," she murmured.

He was beautiful.

Justin went from Ginger's arms into Skip's arms into our mom's arms and, finally, into Francie's arms. She held him like a charm she would cherish forever.

And our bond as sisters just gained a link.

If only Ginger's breast-feeding experience was as easy as her childbirth. She wouldn't put it up there with giving up chocolate, but it was an excruciating endeavor. Her goal was to nurse Justin for his first year of life, as research indicated that breast-fed babies developed fewer childhood diseases and allergies. Justin's fate would not mirror that of his cousin, whose life-threatening peanut allergy had landed him in the ER more than a couple of times.

Yes, Ginger was determined to go the distance—a whole year.

What a lofty goal. She nearly gave up a dozen times

that first month. But thanks to her SOS call to the La Leche Hotline and their unceasing support and guidance, she stuck with it. After all, Justin's healthy start would pay off down the road.

Six months later, still breast-feeding, she knew it was time to start Justin on some select solid foods. Following her pediatrician's guidelines, she avoided high-risk food allergens: milk, nuts, eggs, and even chocolate. Rice cereal topped the "safe food list," and Justin tolerated it well with no allergic reaction. Eventually, she moved onto puréed organic apples, pears, peaches, and spinach. Again, he was fine. Next, plain pasta and chicken were added to his menu. Good, good. It all went so smoothly.

Too smoothly.

Our first rude awakening came on the night we celebrated Justin's first birthday. Carrying a candlelit ice cream cake to the table, we sang:

"Happy birthday to you . . ."

Justin's eyes lit up when Ginger gave him a tiny taste of the vanilla ice cream cake. He was in heaven!

"More," he begged, unaware that his sweet face was already swelling up with hives.

Further inspection revealed his lips were swelling up, too. In panic mode, Ginger called her pediatrician, who told her to give him Benadryl. Within the hour, the swelling was gone, but our nerves were shattered.

The celebration was over.

KIDS IN THE KITCHEN

For safety precautions when cooking with kids, make sure they understand the kitchen drill:

1. Ovens, stovetop burners, pots, and pans in use are HOT.

2. Always use pot holders or oven mitts when handling the above.

3. Pan handles should always point over the stove and not hang over the edge of the counter.

4. No knife handling; all slicing, chopping, mincing, etc., should be performed by an adult.

5. Long hair should be pulled back.

6. Always cook with adult supervision.

PANTRY ITEMS

For recommended name brands for some items listed below, see page 13.

In addition to all the pantry items you normally stock such as all-purpose flour, baking soda and baking powder, olive and vegetable oil, nonstick cooking spray, etc., be sure to always have the following on hand:

Soy milk

Soy creamer

Soy butter

Vegan cheese; all varieties

Dairy-free semisweet chocolate chips

Non-dairy sour cream

Non-dairy cream cheese

Vegan mayonnaise

Dairy-free panko bread crumbs

Vegetable shortening (non-hydrogenated)

Unsweetened applesauce

Tofu

EQUIPMENT USED

Our recipes require very basic equipment:

Pots, small, medium, and large

Pans, small, medium, and large

Bowls, small, medium, and large

Cookie sheets

Baking sheets

Cake pans

Pizza pan

Muffin pans

Handheld or stand mixer

Measuring cups

Measuring spoons

Spatulas

Kitchen thermometer

Food processor

PERSONAL NOTE AND PREFERENCES

Our recipes tend to contain lower sodium than others, by choice. Our father's untimely death at age fifty-six was caused by hypertension, so we've always been conscious of our sodium intake. For example, we don't add salt to pasta water or sprinkle it on at every stage of the cooking process. Truly, we don't believe it's necessary and it only fuels an unnatural desire for more salt.

Also, when cooking, brand names selection is a personal preference. Ours include:

Soy Milk: Silk Soy Milk

Soy Creamer: Silk Soy Creamer

Soy Butter: Earth Balance Soy Butter

Vegan Cheese: Daiya Cheddar Style, Mozzarella Style and Pepper Jack Shreds

Dairy-free Semi-sweet Chocolate Chips: Enjoy Life Semi-sweet Mini Chips

Non-dairy Sour Cream: Tofutti Better Than Sour Cream

Non-dairy Cream Cheese: Tofutti Better Than Cream Cheese

Vegan Mayonnaise: Vegenaise

Bread Crumbs: Ian's Original Panko Bread-crumbs (note: to our knowledge, only the "Original" is dairy-free)

Shortening: Spectrum Organic All Vegetable Shortening (non-hydrogenated)

*J*ustin's first visit to the allergist's office confirmed that it would not be his last. That day, a skin prick test was performed on his forearm. The skin was gently scratched and a minute amount of milk protein was placed into the shallow scratch. Seconds later, a giant red wheal appeared, indicating a severe allergy. It was hard to feel optimistic but we tried.

"So it's just hives we have to worry about, right?" Ginger asked.

The allergist explained to us that Justin's first exposure to dairy caused hives, but the second reaction could very well be more severe. He went on to tell us that the first reaction to an allergen isn't always indicative of a second reaction because sometimes the immune system creates a protein called an antibody that works against a particular food. However, the second exposure to the allergen could very well result in an anaphylactic reaction due to the body releasing chemicals, including histamines, that attack the vital organs.

The allergist asked us if we suspected any other food culprits and Ginger told him that once, after she ate some peanuts, Justin broke out in hives. It was time for more skin testing that revealed more bad news. The list of foods that were possibly life-threatening for Justin turned out to be staggering: dairy, nuts, eggs, sesame, and a host of etceteras. His seasonal allergies fared no better: tree pollen, grasses, ragweed. The antihistamine Atarax was prescribed, along with an EpiPen—short for "Epinephrine Injection"—an auto-injector that helps stop a life-threatening reaction, in case he ever went into anaphylactic shock. Wherever Justin went, so did his medicine bag, stuffed with the likes of Atarax, EpiPen, and Benadryl.

Ginger was a wreck, but she took comfort that the odds were good that Justin might, in time, beat his dairy allergy. After all, his allergist had informed us that 75 percent of children outgrew it by their fifth birthday. So there was hope.

For now, anyway, our chocolate shop was Justin's hazard zone; a mere whiff of chocolate-covered peanuts seemed to make him break out in hives. So much for the proverbial kid in a candy store! Our dream of "breaking chocolate truffles" with our little guy was just that—a dream for now. But we were counting the days.

Up until his second year of preschool, Ginger coasted in the kitchen, serving Justin baked chicken, rice or potatoes, and steamed veggies—bland but supernutritious meals—while we waited for a day we prayed would come, when Justin outgrew his food allergies. In the meantime, a certain reality hovered over her like a slowly darkening sky: What would happen once Justin graduated from half day preschool to all-day kindergarten? What would he eat for lunch?

Apron on, Ginger began experimenting like a mad foodie with dairy-free, nut-free, and egg-free recipes. In her test kitchen, some dishes were admittedly duds, but others were delicious. Who knew fluffy pancakes were possible when you substituted milk and eggs with rice milk and applesauce? Who knew tofu could replace ricotta cheese in an Italian dish? Deprived? Forget about it! Justin was getting nourishment in every sense of the word. With a Hearty Homemade Wheat Bread sandwich tucked in his lunch box, a slice of chocolate chip cake for a party, and Best Beef Stroganoff for supper, his world just got a little brighter.

Sigh.

YUMMY STARTERS

Whether just walking in from a game of tennis or studying for a test, Justin's tummy is always growling long before mealtime. The solution? Starters that are not only hearty, but also "yummy-licious." We don't do a lot of fried cooking, but our starters that sizzle in the pan are worth the guilt. Terrific for tiding over Justin's ever-growing appetite, these can also be mix and matched for a perfectly eclectic meal. Pair Seoulful Half-Moon Dumplings with Mini Potato and Bacon Bites or Scallion 'n' Squash Pancakes with Zesty White Bean Dip with Veggies Galore. Why not?

Seoulful Half-Moon Dumplings

*B*orn from Korean dumplings called *man-doo*, these were inspired by the many platters we made with our mom when we were kids. Her job was to fill a big bowl with diced veggies—cabbage, onion, carrot—along with tofu, ground beef, garlic, sesame oil and seeds, and seasonings so savory and fragrant you just wanted to dig in, which we did, with our hands. Our job was to squish the mixture together until it looked like a giant meatball. After rimming a wonton wrapper with egg wash, the next step was to dollop a small teaspoon of the filling mixture into the wonton center, fold into a triangle, and seal the edges. The art of dimpling the wonton shut was the fun part. Ta-da!

Making dumplings for Justin is just as fun, and when he re-enacts our role of yore—squishing, rimming, dolloping, folding, pressing, dimpling—we grow nostalgic. Neither sesame oil nor sesame seeds are used in this recipe; and the wonton wrappers are sealed with water, not egg wash. But take our word for it, no flavor is sacrificed. Thank goodness our mom, long retired from cooking, is still here to enjoy all the dumplings we make.

Note: The eggless, round wonton wrappers can be found at any Asian market.

DIPPING SAUCE

2 tablespoons soy sauce

1 tablespoon white or rice wine vinegar

1 tablespoon water

¼ teaspoon sugar

Freshly ground black pepper

DUMPLINGS

4 garlic cloves

1 onion

2 large zucchini

½ pound lean ground beef (90/10) or ground chicken breast meat

One 16-ounce package eggless, round wonton wrappers

8 ounces firm tofu

2 teaspoons fresh ginger, peeled and minced

1 tablespoon soy sauce

1 teaspoon sea salt

Freshly ground black pepper

Canola oil, for panfrying

Whisk together all of the ingredients for the dipping sauce. Set aside.

In a food processor, pulse the garlic, onions, and zucchini; transfer to a large bowl. Add the ground beef or chicken, tofu, ginger, soy, salt and pepper and mix by hand.

Line a baking sheet with wax paper. Brush or dip half of each wonton wrapper (on one side) into a small bowl of water, then place a rounded teaspoon of the filling into the center. Fold over the wonton to make a half-moon, seal, then dimple shut. Thinly coat a skillet with 1 table-spoon of canola oil and place over medium heat. Place 10 dumplings in the skillet. When things get sizzling, add 2 tablespoons of water and cover with a lid. Cook about 4 minutes on each side, or until golden brown. Repeat to make the rest of the dumplings.

Yields about 50 dumplings

DUMPLING OPTIONS

Vegetarian Option: For a vegetarian version, add one cup broccoli florets to other veggies in the food processor and substitute an extra 8 ounces of firm tofu for the meat (total tofu for the recipe will be 16 ounces). When we make these for Francie (a vegetarian), she doesn't share!

Steam Option: Set a single layer of dumplings in a steamer, coated with vegetable spray, over a pot of water. Once the water is boiling, steam the dumplings for 15 to 20 minutes.

Freezer Friendly: We always make a hundred dumplings at a time and freeze the dumplings we don't cook in ziplock freezer bags. They are good in the freezer for up to 2 months.

Mini Potato and Bacon Bites

*G*inger's favorite hobby is playing tennis, and when Justin is not taking lessons at the local club, he often joins her on the court. At a recent tennis party Ginger was hosting, her friend Sue brought over a platter of bite-size potato and bacon appetizers. They were gobbled up so fast, Ginger only got one. Yummy.

Since Justin loves potatoes and bacon, and since he is always ravenous after playing tennis, Ginger thought they would make a perfect postgame snack for him. Putting her own spin on Sue's recipe, she went for this sure-fire winner.

12 small potatoes
1 tablespoon olive oil
½ cup vegan mayonnaise
½ cup shredded vegan cheddar cheese
½ cup shredded vegan mozzarella cheese
½ pound bacon, cooked and crumbled
½ cup scallions, minced
2 tablespoons fresh chopped basil (or 2 teaspoons dried)

Preheat the oven to 400°F.

Rub the potatoes with olive oil, and place on an ungreased baking sheet. Bake for 45 minutes, or until fork-tender. Cool the potatoes.

Cut the potatoes in half, then slice a thin sliver from the bottom of each to help them stand. Scoop out the potato pulp, leaving about a ¼-inch shell around the sides. Reserve the pulp.

Stir together the reserved potato pulp, vegan mayonnaise, vegan cheeses, bacon, scallions, and basil. Spoon mixture equally among the potato shells.

Broil for 3 to 5 minutes until lightly browned. Serve warm.

Yields 24 bites

Tzatziki

Our shop manager, fondly known as "Koomo," was planning to spend the Fourth of July with us at Ginger's house. Of Greek descent, Koomo had been telling us all week long he was preparing "a surprise" Justin could enjoy. He was especially excited because the surprise would include some of his home-grown cucumbers.

On the Fourth, Koomo came over toting pita chips and veggie sticks, along with a bowl of something creamy-looking. "It's tzatziki," he pronounced, proudly.

An aromatic Greek yogurt dip chock-full of garlic and cucumber, Koomo had simply substituted soy yogurt for the usual dairy yogurt. Given its pungent nature, we were thrilled that Justin was willing to dip a pita chip into the tzatziki.

"It's good."

But Ginger could read Justin's mind. Something's missing. There are times when simple substitutions just won't do the trick. While soy yogurt is great, it doesn't quite possess the same creaminess as dairy yogurt. The next day in the test kitchen we combined non-dairy soy yogurt and non-dairy sour cream, which is as creamy as the real stuff . . . and voilà! It worked like magic! After one bite, Justin was spellbound and exclaimed: "It's unbelievable!"

1 cup soy yogurt

1 cup non-dairy sour cream

3 tablespoons olive oil

1 tablespoon white vinegar

3 garlic cloves, minced

½ teaspoon sea salt

¼ teaspoon freshly ground black pepper

2 medium cucumbers, peeled, seeded, and diced

2 teaspoons chopped fresh dill

A few sprigs of fresh dill, for garnish (optional)

In a medium bowl, combine the soy yogurt and non-dairy sour cream. Set aside. In a small bowl, combine the olive oil, vinegar, garlic, salt, and pepper and mix well with a fork. Add the olive oil mixture to the yogurt–sour cream mixture and mix until creamy. Add the cucumber and chopped fresh dill. Garnish with sprigs of fresh dill, if desired. Chill for 2 hours before serving.

Enjoy this with dairy-free pita wedges or chips, toasted French bread, and veggie sticks. Delicious as a sandwich spread, too!

Yields 3 cups dip

Note: Tzatziki tastes even better if you let the flavors meld together overnight in the refrigerator. Garnish with dill, if using, just before serving.

Tater and Chive Cakes

With crackers, chives, and a quick stir, leftover mashed potatoes can easily morph into these Tater and Chive Cakes, so irresistible we gobble up most of them straight off the griddle. Sometimes the joy of cooking is truly the joy of cooking, and what a party we have! The few cakes that make it to the dinner table are for Justin's dad and grandmother—by then, we're so full we can't look at another one!

3 large potatoes, peeled and sliced

½ cup soy milk

3 tablespoons soy butter

1 teaspoon sea salt

2 cups crushed Original Premium Saltines or Whole Foods 365 Crackers or any other similar dairy-free crackers

2 garlic cloves, minced

½ teaspoon freshly ground black pepper

½ cup finely chopped fresh chives, 1 tablespoon reserved for the non-dairy sour cream

Canola oil, for panfrying

1 cup non-dairy sour cream

Place potatoes in a large pot of cold water and bring to a boil. Cook until soft. Drain the potatoes and transfer to a mixing bowl. Add soy milk, soy butter, and salt. Using an electric mixer, whip the ingredients together until combined. Add the crackers, garlic, pepper, and chives and hand mix well.

Preheat a skillet, thinly coated with canola oil, over medium-high heat. Form 2½-inch patties and fry for about 3 minutes per side, or until golden brown. Whip the reserved chives into the non-dairy sour cream and serve on the side.

Yields about 30 cakes

Zesty White Bean Dip with Veggies Galore

One night during the holidays, we were all invited to dinner at our brother Sam's house where the spread of hors d'oeuvre was a mile long. Justin asked his aunt Francie about the creamy dip next to the pita chips.

"That's hummus, honey."

"Can I have some?"

Like most kids with nut allergies, Justin has to avoid legumes as well, including lentils, peas, and the culprit here, chickpeas.

"No, Justin. Sorry." To his brave nod, she added, "But I bet your mom can whip up something just as tasty."

"Really?"

Fortunately, the earth is populated with many beans Justin can eat—kidney beans, black beans, pinto beans, to name a few—so a bean dip seemed like a natural fit.

Made with white beans, lemon juice, and a touch of vegan mayo, Ginger's alternative to hummus is healthy, high in protein, and disappears before your eyes.

One 15- to 16-ounce can cannellini beans, drained

1 garlic clove, minced

⅛ cup olive oil

2 tablespoons vegan mayonnaise

2 tablespoons freshly squeezed lemon juice

2 sprigs fresh dill

Sea salt

Freshly ground black pepper

In a food processor, pulse the beans, garlic, olive oil, vegan mayo, lemon juice, and dill together until creamy. Season with salt and pepper to taste. Serve with veggies. This is also great with dairy-free pita wedges, tortilla chips, water crackers, and wheat toast.

Yields 1 cup dip

Scallion 'n' Squash Pancakes

With the exception of sesame and egg, Korean dishes are often free of high-allergy foods. In our Scallion 'n' Squash Pancakes recipe, cornstarch replaces egg, and of course you won't see any sign of sesame oil or seeds. Considered an appetizer, these pancakes are crispy on the outside, moist and chewy on the inside, and so irresistible they're prone to trump the rest of the meal. Sometimes we make entrée portions and serve with a side of rice.

DIPPING SAUCE

2 tablespoons soy sauce

1 tablespoon white or rice wine vinegar

1 tablespoon water

¼ teaspoon sugar

Freshly ground black pepper

PANCAKES

1 cup all-purpose flour, presifted

2 tablespoons cornstarch

½ cup water plus 4 tablespoon water

2 scallions, sliced into 2-inch-long pieces

¼ cup grated green squash

¾ teaspoon sea salt

¼ teaspoon crushed red pepper flakes (optional)

Canola oil, for panfrying

Whisk together all of the ingredients for the dipping sauce. Set aside.

With a large spoon, mix together all of the ingredients except for the canola oil. Preheat a large skillet with the oil over medium-high heat. Make 3 pancakes at a time, using ¼ cup of batter per pancake. Cook for 2 to 3 minutes on each side, or until the edges turn lightly golden brown and crispy. Serve immediately with the dipping sauce.

Yields 6 pancakes

The moment of truth had arrived: Justin was ready to be tested again. With hope in our hearts, we had diligently followed his allergist's guidelines by avoiding Justin's food allergens the past two years. Perhaps by now, he was allergy-free.

Wishful thinking.

Along with milk, Justin was skin-prick tested for seventeen other allergens, including peanuts, eggs, soy, dogs, cats, dust mites, corn, sesame, oak, and grass. He was a very unhappy camper, weeping each time they pricked his tiny back. It was difficult to watch him go through this agony at his tender age, and so unfair. Like his previous tests, within seconds, each prick resulted in a red wheal, some bigger than others. By the end of the test, his back was covered with seventeen wheals. Once again, he was labeled a severely allergic child. The only non-allergic or negative reaction was to horse dander.

While the skin test indicated that Justin was allergic to soy and corn, Ginger told the allergist that her son seemed to tolerate both without any symptoms.

"Allergy testing isn't always a science," the doctor explained. We had no idea how many times we would hear this statement in years to come.

We were heartbroken.

In the car on the way home from the doctor's office, Justin announced: "You know what I want for Christmas this year?"

"What, Mister?" Skip said at the wheel.

Ginger, holding back her tears, turned around and looked at her beautiful son as he shouted: "A horse!"

Justin was too young to grasp the full meaning of his test results, but his three-year-old fortitude taught us that acceptance was a vital part of positively dealing with his food allergies. It also meant it was time to re-stock the allergen-free pantry.

ULTIMATE SIDES

A side dish can be as simple as a green salad or a bowl of sweet corn. But here are some sides for when you're in the mood for a bit more wow. Make Quick and Easy "Cheezy" Sausage Biscuits and Creamy Dreamy Mashed Potatoes for oohs, aahs, and applause. Make Rock Star Onion Rings, and your whole family will treat you like a rock star!

Rock Star Onion Rings

While neither of us are junk food lovers, we're both cooking show junkies, and once in a while we can't help but crave a greasy spoon specialty. One night Francie called us while tuned into The Food Network's *Diners, Drive-Ins and Dives*. The host, Guy Fieri, was eating onion rings in the kitchen of Village Cafe in Richmond. Salivating, she wondered: Could we fashion onion rings for Justin without the usual eggs and buttermilk? But of course! These Rock Star Onion Rings are thinly sliced and fried to perfection in a flash.

1½ cups all-purpose flour plus 1 cup of flour for coating the onion rings

1¾ cups soy milk

1 teaspoon garlic powder

1 teaspoon sea salt

Freshly ground black pepper

2 tablespoons cornstarch

2 tablespoons water

1 large Vidalia or Spanish onion, thinly sliced (about ¼ inch thick) and separated

About 1 quart canola oil

1 cup dairy-free panko bread crumbs

In a medium pot, heat the oil to 370°F.

In a large bowl, combine the 1½ cups flour, soy milk, garlic powder, salt, pepper, cornstarch, and water. Set the batter aside.

Place the onion slices and the 1 cup of flour in a large ziplock bag. Shake to coat. Place the bread crumbs into a shallow dish. Dip a few onion rings at a time into the batter and dip the wet rings into the bread crumbs.

When the oil is to temperature, deep-fry for 2 minutes, or until golden brown. Drain on paper towels.

Yields about 25 onion rings

Vegan Potato Salad

T his salad is light and lively with vegan mayonnaise and contains more raw veggies than traditional potato salad. Another plus: You can pack this up as a worry-free side for a picnic lunch. Without egg-based mayo, it has a longer "shelf" life.

8 red potatoes, cut into ½-inch cubes
1 cup diced carrots
1 cup sliced celery
1 cup diced dill pickles
⅔ cup vegan mayonnaise

2 tablespoons Dijon mustard
¼ cup pickle juice
1 rounded teaspoon dried dill weed
Sea salt
Freshly ground black pepper

In a large pot of water, boil the potatoes, covered, until tender. Put the carrots, celery, and pickles into a large bowl. Drain the potatoes and run briefly under cold water until cool, making sure the excess water has drained from the potatoes before adding them to the bowl of vegetables. Add the vegan mayonnaise, Dijon mustard, pickle juice, dill weed, and salt and pepper to taste. Mix thoroughly. Serve at room temperature or chilled.

Yields 6 servings

Creamy Dreamy Mashed Potatoes

a family favorite, this satisfying side dish is great mashed rustic style or whipped smooth. Top with bacon bits or thinly sliced scallions, if desired.

6 medium Yukon Gold or
    new potatoes, sliced
    ¼ inch thick
½ cup soy milk
¾ cup non-dairy sour cream

¼ cup soy butter
Sea salt
Freshly ground black pepper
Bacon bits or sliced scallions,
    for garnish (optional)

In a large pot of water, boil the potatoes until tender, about 25 minutes. Drain and transfer the potatoes to a large bowl. Add the soy milk and mash or beat until smooth. Add the non-dairy sour cream and soy butter and mix in with a spoon. Season with salt and pepper to taste. Garnish with bacon bits or scallions. if desired.

Yields 4 servings

Best Biscuits Ever

Perfect with jam, chutney, or soy butter—although Justin loves to clean his bowl of White Bean Turkey Chili with these light, flaky biscuits. His smile is our reward.

2 cups all-purpose flour
1 tablespoon baking
     powder
½ teaspoon salt
1 tablespoon sugar

⅓ cup soy butter or
     vegetable shortening,
     preferably non-
     hydrogenated
1 cup soy milk

Preheat the oven to 425°F.

In a medium bowl, whisk together all of the dry ingredients. Using a fork, cut in the soy butter or shortening until the mixture is crumbly. Slowly stir in the milk until the dough mixture pulls away from the sides of the bowl. Knead for 1 minute on a floured surface.

Roll out the dough to a thickness of 1 inch. Using a round cookie cutter or a glass rim, cut out biscuits, approximately 2½ inches in diameter and place on an ungreased baking sheet. Bake for 10 to 12 minutes until golden brown.

Yields about 12 biscuits

Quick and Easy
"Cheezy" Sausage Biscuits

With a tall glass of calcium-fortified orange juice, these biscuits work as a nice, well-rounded breakfast.

5 frozen precooked turkey sausage links

1 tablespoon olive oil

2 cups Heart Smart Bisquick

1 teaspoon garlic powder

1 teaspoon freshly ground black pepper

2 tablespoons soy butter, chopped into small pieces

¼ cup chopped fresh basil

½ cup soy milk

1 cup shredded vegan cheddar cheese

Preheat the oven to 400°F. Coat a 12-well muffin pan with nonstick cooking spray.

Thaw the sausage links in the microwave. In a skillet over medium-high heat, warm the olive oil. Add the sausages and brown on all sides. Set aside to cool. When cooled, slice into ½-inch pieces. Set aside.

In a medium bowl, combine the Bisquick, garlic

powder, and pepper. Add the butter, basil, and soy milk. Mix until the ingredients are wet and lumpy. Add the sliced sausage and shredded cheese. Fill the prepared muffin cups. Bake for 10 to 12 minutes until golden brown.

Yields 12 biscuits

A Midsummer's Day Creamy Tomato-Basil Soup

For us, this beautiful, Crayola-colored soup is a side that becomes a meal—no entrée necessary.

Of course, our family isn't exactly known for our delicate appetites—one bowl does not make a meal! Marching up to the stove for second and third servings is how we roll.

6 tablespoons soy butter

2 slices bacon, finely chopped

1 Vidalia onion, chopped

5 baby carrots, chopped

1 large celery stalk, chopped

5 garlic cloves, minced

⅓ cup all-purpose flour

4 cups low-sodium chicken broth

One 28-ounce can whole, peeled tomatoes, with their juices

1 cup chopped fresh basil

¼ cup chopped parsley

1 teaspoon dried thyme

1 cup soy creamer

1¾ teaspoons kosher salt

Freshly ground black pepper

Melt the butter in a large soup pot over medium-high heat. Add the bacon and cook, stirring, until crispy.

Transfer the bacon to a paper towel–lined plate and set aside. Lower the heat to medium, and add the onion, carrots, celery, and garlic. Cook, covered, stirring occasionally until the vegetables are soft, about 5 minutes. Add the flour and cook, stirring constantly, until creamy, about 2 minutes.

Pour in the broth and the tomatoes with their juices. Bring to a boil, whisking constantly. Add the basil, parsley, and thyme. Lower the heat and simmer for 20 to 25 minutes. Remove from the heat and let cool.

Once cooled, transfer the chunky soup mixture to a large bowl. Ladle half of the soup into a blender and purée, then pour it back into the pot. Repeat with the remaining half. Reheat the puréed soup, add the soy creamer, and season with salt and pepper to taste. Serve with Spicy Savory Crackers (page 129).

Yields 6 servings

Hearty Potato Soup

For some reason, making soup always feels like a labor of love, and Hearty Potato Soup is no exception. You feel it in the stirring, knowing this is for someone very special. Your reward? Bring this bowl o' chunky goodness to the table and watch your child's face light up.

Soup's on!

1 pound reduced-fat bacon, chopped
2 celery stalks, diced
1 onion, chopped
4 garlic cloves, minced
4 large russet potatoes, peeled and cubed

4 cups chicken broth
4 tablespoons soy butter
¼ cup all-purpose flour
1 cup soy creamer
1 teaspoon dried tarragon
Sea salt
Freshly ground black pepper

In a large pot, cook the bacon over medium heat until crispy. Remove the bacon from the pot, and set aside. Drain off two-thirds of the bacon grease.

In the remaining bacon grease, sauté the celery and

onion until the onion is translucent. Add the garlic, and continue cooking for a few minutes. Add the cubed potatoes and toss until the potatoes are coated with the bacon grease. Sauté for about 5 minutes. Crumble the bacon and return it to the pot. Add the chicken broth, cover, and simmer until the potatoes are tender.

In a small pan, melt the soy butter over medium heat. Stir in the flour and continue to stir until creamy. Stir in the soy creamer and tarragon. Bring the mixture to a boil and stir until thickened. Remove from the heat. Stir the mixture into the potato soup. Ladle half of the soup into a blender and pulse a few times just until creamy; don't overblend or the mixture will be glutinous. Season to taste with salt and plenty of pepper. This soup is perfect served with a simple salad.

Yields 8 servings

ALLERGY REPORT 2003
AGE: FIVE

Justin was old enough to dress himself that morning we were returning to the allergist's office. Despite the statistics we'd heard—that 75 percent of kids outgrow their milk allergy by age five—and despite the fact he was flourishing developmentally, we went in with low expectations. Sure enough, nothing had changed; Justin was still allergic to milk, nuts, eggs, and more. Of course, we were a little disappointed, but we had no choice but to accept this reality: Justin was an allergic child, and we could live with that. We could also continue creating more allergen-free recipes in our kitchen. By now, we had nearly enough for a cookbook!

MARVELOUS ENTRÉES

From our Best Beef Stroganoff to Home-made "Mac 'n' Cheeze" with a Twist, from our Emperor's Tempura to White Bean Turkey Chili, from our Dreamy Broccoli Risotto to "Chubby Cheezy" Quesadillas, your child—and whole family—will freak out over how fantastic allergen-free cooking can be.

Pizza by Justin

Justin's elementary school planned an end-of-the-year bash in the school's courtyard, and pizza and punch were on the menu. Though he had watched his mom make pizza before, this time—after all, he was a big guy now, graduating from the sixth grade—Justin decided to assemble his own pièce de résistance himself. He wiped down the kitchen counter, floured it, then rolled out the dough like a regular ol' Mario. After spooning on the pizza sauce, he piled on a combo of vegan cheeses, then topped it with pepperoni rounds. Frankly, it looked more like a pizza mountain than a pizza pie as it went into the oven.

Now Justin often prepares his own pizzas; and when we can talk him into making an extra pie, it's pizza party time for all—and that's *amore!*

Brooklyn Style Pizza Dough, available in the frozen food section at Whole Foods, is outstanding, and makes the whole pizza-making process more kid-friendly. But fear not, if you can't find this frozen dough near you, we've included a terrific pizza dough recipe as well.

One 16-ounce frozen Brooklyn Style Pizza Dough (follow directions to thaw)

1 tablespoon extra virgin olive oil

½ to ¾ cup favorite pizza sauce (check ingredients for possible allergens), as desired

Pepperoni slices (optional)

1 cup shredded vegan cheddar cheese

1 cup shredded vegan mozzarella cheese

Garlic powder

Preheat the oven to 450°F.

Spread the pizza crust with the desired amount of pizza sauce. Top with pepperoni, if using. Scatter the vegan cheddar and mozzarella cheeses over the top. Top with another layer of pepperoni, if using. Sprinkle with garlic powder.

Bake for 10 to 12 minutes until the crust is golden brown.

Homemade Thick and Chewy Pizza Dough

*D*efrost dough when ready to use. Remove dough from packaging. Lightly cover dough with 1 tablespoon of extra virgin olive oil and place in a large bowl. Cover with plastic wrap and let thaw at room temperature for 6 hours.

Your pizza dough crust is a canvas for your imagination. Just about any topping you see on your pizza carryout menu will work: onions, mushrooms, peppers, broccoli, black olives, etc. Go Hawaiian with pineapple and ham chunks. Go Tex-Mex with corn and green chili peppers. Be daring and go Korean—long before "Kimchi Pizza" was a hit in Queens, New York, our mom was adding the spicy dish to her pizza.

2½ cups all-purpose flour	1½ teaspoons active dry yeast
1 teaspoon sea salt	½ cups pastry flour
1½ cups water	Olive oil

In a large bowl, mix the 2½ cups all-purpose flour with the salt, water, and yeast. Mix in the pastry flour until the dough is slightly sticky. Knead for 15 minutes on a floured surface until smooth. Place the dough into a large flour-dusted bowl. Cover with plastic wrap. Store in the refrigerator for at least 7 hours.

Punch the dough down and divide it in half. Roll out the dough on a floured surface to fit a 12½-inch diameter pizza pan. Place on a pizza pan. Add the toppings, and brush the edges of the pizza with olive oil.

Yields 2 pizza crusts

Note: For best results, prepare this dough in the morning for dinner in the evening.

"Chubby Cheezy" Quesadillas

In elementary school, when Justin had birthday party plans, Ginger would make a batch of allergen-free cupcakes and pack one to go so he could proudly eat cake, too. But one time, he was invited to celebrate a friend's birthday at a Mexican restaurant, which meant cheesy tacos and enchiladas, dishes off-limits to him. Normally Ginger would try to prepare a Mexican alternative he could enjoy but, since we were deep into the Christmas season at our chocolate shop, there was little time. So she packed a roasted turkey sandwich for him, all the while fretting over two things: one, the possibility of cross contamination at the restaurant, what with kids and their sticky fingers; and two, that Justin would feel like the odd kid out, eating a sandwich while his buddies were devouring nacho platters.

In the car on the way home, he insisted he had a

good time. Justin was no whiner, but, staring out the window, his spirit seemed a bit glum.

"Mommy, what were those triangles my friends were eating?"

"They're called quesadillas."

"They looked really good."

In the rearview mirror, Ginger gave him a wink. "Yeah? Well, they're not as good as the ones we'll make."

Over the holiday break, we created our own quesadillas, cut into perfectly toasted triangles—as easy to make as any sandwich. A layer of non-dairy cream cheese serves to seal the quesadilla and make it puff up while cooking, keeping the center intact until sliced.

1 pound boneless, skinless thin-sliced chicken breast fillets

2 tablespoons soy sauce

2 garlic cloves, minced

1 large onion, thinly sliced

1 tablespoon olive oil

8 ounces non-dairy cream cheese

12 ounces vegan mozzarella cheese, shredded

2 tablespoons chopped fresh basil

6 medium, soft flour tortillas (check ingredients for possible allergens)

1 teaspoon canola oil per tortilla

4 plum tomatoes, chopped (optional)

2 avocados, pitted, peeled, and chopped (optional)

½ cup non-dairy sour cream (optional)

In a large bowl, combine the chicken, soy sauce, garlic, onion, and olive oil. Mix well and marinate for 30 minutes.

Preheat the oven to 350°F.

Transfer the chicken with the marinade to a baking pan and cook in the oven for 30 minutes. Set aside to cool.

In a bowl, combine the non-dairy cream cheese, vegan mozzarella cheese, and basil and set aside.

Reserving the juices, hand-shred the cooled chicken into a bowl, then pour the reserved juices back over the chicken.

For each tortilla, spread the cheese mixture from edge to edge. Next spread one-sixth of the shredded chicken and onion across the tortilla, leaving a ½-inch border for sealing the tortilla. Fold over the tortilla and seal.

Thinly coat a large skillet with about a teaspoon of canola oil and place over medium heat. Cook the tortillas, one at a time, until golden brown on each side. When cooled, slice into 3 triangles. If desired, serve with chopped tomatoes, avocados, and non-dairy sour cream.

Yields 6 servings

Variation: For an Asian version, delete the chicken breasts, soy sauce, olive oil, and garlic and substitute Grandma's Bulgogi (page 96). Voilà—Korean Quesadillas! For a barbecue version, delete those same ingredients and substitute precooked barbecued baby back ribs. You can find them at the grocery store, jet-packed in plastic wrap, and dairy-free (but please always check the label).

Mother Earth's Cream Sauce
for Rice or Pasta

*a*s every parent knows, it takes time and patience to encourage their child to eat their "Five a Day"—five servings of fruits and vegetables—and even though Justin's diet allowed him to eat many fruits and veggies to his heart's content, he was no exception. However, once we asked him to help us with the gardening, earth's bounties slowly began to look different to him. He dug his hands into pots of soil and planted himself into the whole experience. Admittedly, he wasn't particularly taken with the basil and chives, but the flowering plum tomato vines were nothing short of magical to him. When the first flowers blossomed into little green tomatoes, he waited patiently for them to turn red and be ready to pick so he could eat them.

This is our allergen-free, vegan variation of rose, or *rosa,* sauce, and was often on Justin's summer menu. In lieu of heavy cream, the low-fat soy creamer (not to mention using herbs from our own pots) makes the dining experience richer for him. Serve this over pasta or rice.

6 tablespoons soy butter
1 onion, thinly sliced
2 garlic cloves, minced
10 plum tomatoes, diced (see Note)
Fresh basil, coarsely chopped (a big bunch or a large fistful)

Fresh parsley, coarsely chopped (a half-bunch or a small fistful)
1 tablespoon sugar
⅔ cup soy creamer
Sea salt
Freshly ground black pepper

In a skillet, melt the butter. Add the onion and garlic and sauté until soft, 10 to 15 minutes.

Add the chopped tomatoes, basil, parsley, and sugar to the skillet and simmer for 25 to 30 minutes until the mixture has a sauce-like consistency.

Add the soy creamer and simmer for 5 minutes more. Season with salt and pepper to taste.

Yields 4 servings

Note: Peeling the tomatoes is optional, depending on whether you enjoy the texture and rustic look of tomato skins, as we do.

Simply Pasta 'n' Beans

Cannellini beans were put on this earth to make dishes creamy, nutritious, and delicious. This bowl of goodness is made with five ingredients and can be whipped up in minutes. For Justin, it was literally love at first bite, and, for a time, simply nothing else would do for supper.

8 ounces fusilli pasta

One 12-ounce can cannellini beans, top liquid drained, but reserve the rest

3 tablespoons soy butter

1 tablespoon soy sauce

Freshly ground black pepper

In a large pot of boiling water, cook the pasta until al dente, no more than 11 minutes. Drain the pasta and transfer to a medium bowl.

Add the cannellini beans with the reserved liquid, the soy butter, soy sauce, and pepper. Mix well to combine. Serve warm.

Yields 4 servings

Variation: Sliced-up turkey sausage links are a wonderful addition to this dish.

Creamy "Cheezy" & Maple Turkey Sausage Pasta

𝒶 crème de la crème, melt-in-your-mouth pasta— our family fights over second servings! This is perfect paired with an arugula and tomato salad, drizzled with a citrus-infused olive oil dressing.

8 ounces thick spaghettini or linguini

6 frozen precooked maple turkey sausage links

1 tablespoon olive oil

2 garlic cloves, minced

10 ounces vegan mozzarella cheese, shredded

Freshly ground black pepper

2 tablespoons chopped fresh parsley

¼ teaspoon crushed red pepper flakes (optional)

In a large pot of boiling water, cook the pasta until al dente, no more than 10 minutes. Meanwhile, defrost the sausage in the microwave. Dice the sausage.

In a skillet over medium-high heat, warm the olive oil. Add minced garlic and the sausage and cook for about 2 minutes. Remove from the heat. Add the drained pasta, vegan mozzarella cheese, black pepper, parsley, and pepper flakes, if you want to add a kick! Mix well to combine. Serve immediately.

Yields 4 servings

Dreamy Broccoli Risotto

With a Korean grandmother who always had a pot of rice cooking at a moment's notice, Justin had an early introduction to the world's most popular grain. And he loved stirring soy butter into his bowl of rice until it was rich and creamy. We share a humorous memory: As a little boy in his bib, Justin would often make us show him how much rice was left in the pot, as if he needed assurance there was enough for several more servings. A decade or so later, we introduced him to risotto in this more complex dish. By then he was no longer a little boy, and no longer asked to see how much was left in the pot; however, he still asked for seconds and thirds.

2 tablespoons olive oil

3 tablespoons soy butter

½ large sweet onion, finely chopped

4 garlic cloves, minced

1½ cups Arborio rice

½ cup dry white wine

2 tablespoons freshly squeezed lemon juice

5 cups hot chicken broth

1 cup soy creamer

3 cups broccoli florets, cooked

2 tablespoons chopped fresh chives

¼ cup shredded vegan mozzarella cheese

¼ cup shredded vegan cheddar cheese

Sea salt

Freshly ground black pepper

Heat the olive oil and soy butter in a large, heavy-bottomed saucepan over medium-high heat. Add the onion and garlic and cook, stirring, until the onion begins to turn golden brown on the edges, about 2 minutes. Pour in the rice, and stir until the rice is coated in the oil and butter and has started to toast, 3 to 4 minutes. Reduce the heat to medium, and stir in the white wine and lemon juice. Cook, stirring, until the wine has almost evaporated. Stir in one-third of the chicken broth and continue to cook, stirring, until incorporated. Repeat this process twice more, stirring constantly; the broth-stirring process should take a total of 15 to 20 minutes. Stir in the soy creamer and cook 5 minutes, then stir in the broccoli, chives, and vegan mozzarella and cheddar cheeses. Cook, stirring, until the risotto is hot and the cheeses have melted. Season to taste with salt and pepper and serve.

Yields 4 servings

Plate-Size Puffy Pancakes

With an allergic child, going to IHOP doesn't exactly figure into our weekend plans. But with a recipe like this up our sleeves, who cares about restaurant pancakes? Our homemade version—without butter, eggs, or milk—can be made in a pinch and is every bit as tempting.

¾ cup vanilla soy milk

2 tablespoons white vinegar

¼ cup unsweetened apple-sauce

1 tablespoon soy butter, melted

1¼ cups all-purpose flour

2 tablespoons sugar

1 teaspoon baking powder

1 teaspoon baking soda

½ teaspoon sea salt

Soy butter, maple syrup, jam, or preserves, for serving

In a medium bowl, combine the soy milk and vinegar. Allow to sour for 5 minutes. Mix in the applesauce and melted soy butter.

In a large bowl, combine the flour, sugar, baking powder, baking soda, and salt.

Pour the liquid mixture over the dry mixture and stir until well incorporated.

Place a skillet, coated with nonstick cooking spray, over medium heat. Ladle in 1/2 cup of batter per pancake. Add fruit chunks, berries, or chocolate chips, if desired (see variation below). Cook until holes appear in the top of the pancake, then flip and cook on the opposite sides, about 3 minutes per side.

Yields 4 large pancakes

Variation: If desired, either mix garnishes such as fruit chunks, berries, or chocolate chips into the batter, or layer on top of already cooked pancakes. Justin likes chocolate chips stirred into the batter.

To top off your pancakes, choose soy butter and/or maple syrup, jam, or preserves— just be sure to check the labels for possible allergens!

Best Beef Stroganoff

The idea for this meal came about when Justin was in the seventh grade, learning about Russia's invasion by Germany in World War II. Suddenly he wanted to know about all things Russian, even the food they ate.

"Beef Stroganoff?" he said, hope in his voice. After all, he knew he wasn't allergic to beef.

Back in the '60s and '70s, our mom occasionally experimented with Western dishes, with limited success. How could we forget her Hungarian Goulash phase, her Canned Fruit in Jell-O phase, her Tuna Boat phase? Thankfully, among the mishaps, was her Beef Stroganoff phase. The cream-colored sauce was rich and flavorful over rice or noodles, dotted with specks of black pepper. It was delicious.

"It's a dish I think we can make," Ginger said. "Let's ask Grandma what goes into it."

Our mom, who lives with Ginger's family, still had the recipe filed in her memory and it called for only one ingredient substitution, sour cream. So simple!

½ pound top sirloin beef steak

4 cups reduced-sodium beef broth

¼ cup dry sherry

8 ounces canned mushrooms, sliced and drained

1 teaspoon freshly ground black pepper

2 teaspoons sea salt

3 tablespoons cornstarch

½ cup water

1 cup non-dairy sour cream

Cooked rice or eggless noodles, for serving

Chopped scallions, for garnish (optional)

Slice the meat into 1 inch long × ¼-inch-thick pieces. Place the pieces into a large pot and pour the beef broth over the meat. Place in the refrigerator for 1 hour.

Over medium heat, bring the meat and broth to a boil. Simmer for 45 minutes. Using a skimmer, remove the excess beef fat foam that rises to the surface of the broth. Add the sherry, mushrooms, pepper, and salt. Cook for 15 minutes more. Add the cornstarch to ½ cup of water and stir well. Add the slurry to the beef broth, stirring constantly until it has thickened. Remove from the heat. Stir in the non-dairy sour cream. Serve immediately over rice or noodles. Garnish with chopped scallions, if desired.

Yields 6 servings

Chunky Chicken Potpie

We like to think of all of the food we make for Justin as "comfort food," but on a winter's day nothing can beat a bubbling potpie browning in the oven. The aroma, like a fire crackling and snow falling, fills us with a warm, homey feeling, and thoughts of the comforting meal to come, a generous plate of Chunky Chicken Potpie.

A good-quality dairy-free piecrust, available in the frozen-food section of most grocery stores, cuts down on the labor of this hearty dish, chock-full of chicken, carrots, peas, and celery.

1 pound boneless, skinless
    chicken breasts, cut
    into ½-inch cubes
⅔ cup sliced carrots
⅔ cup frozen peas
⅔ cup sliced celery
⅓ cup soy butter
½ cup chopped onion
2 large garlic cloves,
    minced
⅓ cup all-purpose flour

½ teaspoon sea salt
½ teaspoon freshly ground
    black pepper
½ teaspoon dried rosemary
½ teaspoon dried thyme
1¾ cups chicken broth
⅔ cup soy milk
2 store-bought dairy-free
    9-inch unbaked
    piecrusts

Preheat the oven to 425°F.

In a saucepan, combine the chicken, carrots, peas, and celery. Add water to cover and bring to a boil. Reduce the heat and simmer for 20 minutes. Remove the chicken mixture from the heat and drain. Set aside.

In the same saucepan, melt the soy butter, add the onion and garlic and cook over medium heat until soft. Stir in the flour, salt, pepper, rosemary, and thyme. Slowly stir in the chicken broth and soy milk. Simmer over medium-low heat until the sauce has thickened. Remove the sauce from the heat and set aside to cool slightly. Place the reserved chicken mixture in the bottom piecrust. Pour the sauce over the chicken mixture. Cover with the top crust, and seal the edges. Make four slits in the top of the pie to allow the steam to escape.

Bake for about 30 minutes, or until golden brown. Let cool for 15 minutes. Serve warm.

Yields 4 servings

White Bean Turkey Chili

*J*ustin's a big football fan. Whether he's watching Sunday football with his dad, or has just come inside from a game of flag football with his friends, this White Bean Turkey Chili, packed with lean protein, really hits the spot.

Spoon up your chili and serve with our Oh-So-Sweet Corn Bread Muffins (page 168) or Best Biscuits Ever (page 46), or both!

1 pound ground turkey breast meat

2 tablespoons olive oil

2 green chili peppers, such as jalapeño peppers, finely chopped

1 large onion, chopped

6 garlic cloves, minced

1¼ tablespoons chili powder

2 cups chicken broth

6 plum tomatoes, diced

Three 15-ounce cans cannellini beans, drained

1 tablespoon sugar

2 tablespoons soy butter

Freshly ground black pepper

Non-dairy sour cream

In a sauté pan over medium heat, brown the ground turkey until no longer pink. Set aside. In a large pot over medium, heat the olive oil. Add the green chilis, onion, and garlic and sauté until soft. Add the chili powder and cook briefly. Add the chicken broth, ground turkey, tomatoes, beans, and sugar. Bring to a boil and simmer for about 30 minutes. Stir in the soy butter. Season to taste with salt and pepper. Serve with a hearty dollop of non-dairy sour cream.

Yields 6 servings

Homemade "Mac 'n' Cheeze" with a Twist

One Saturday, Justin's dad Skip was making macaroni 'n' cheese from a box for a quick lunch—again. The orange powder caught Justin's eye—again.

"That looks like Kool-Aid, Dad."

His dad chuckled. "A modern invention of man, son. Cheese powder."

Ginger shuddered.

"How can you eat that, Skip?" Francie teased him.

"Old habits die hard," he said, stirring the pot. "I grew up on this stuff."

"When I was your age, Justin," Francie remembered, "my friend's mom used to make us real macaroni and cheese. When it came out of the oven, it was still bubbling."

Already Ginger was checking her pantry and fridge

for ingredients, and, in no time, we were recreating the macaroni of Francie's youth. In lieu of elbow macaroni, Ginger used fusilli pasta, whose corkscrew shape makes it great for saucy dishes.

The casserole emerged from the oven all creamy and cheesy, with browned panko bread crumbs on top. Ginger spooned a test portion onto her son's plate. He dug in and polished it off in no time.

"More, please."

He never asked about his dad's boxed version again.

8 ounces fusilli pasta

¼ cup soy butter plus 3 tablespoons soy butter (for crumb topping)

3 tablespoons all-purpose flour

2 cups soy milk

8 ounces non-dairy cream cheese

½ teaspoon garlic powder

¼ teaspoon sea salt

½ teaspoon freshly ground black pepper

3 teaspoons Dijon mustard

8 ounces vegan cheddar cheese, shredded

1 cup dairy-free panko bread crumbs

3 tablespoons chopped fresh parsley

Preheat the oven to 400°F.

In a large pot of boiling water, cook the pasta for 10 to 12 minutes, or until al dente. Drain the pasta.

Meanwhile, in a large saucepan over medium heat, melt the ¼ cup of soy butter. Slowly stir in the flour and cook until bubbly. Mix in the soy milk, non-dairy cream cheese, garlic powder, salt, pepper, and mustard. Cook until smooth and thick.

Mix in the cooked fusilli and vegan cheddar cheese. Pour the mixture into a 9 × 11-inch casserole dish.

Combine 3 tablespoons soy butter, the panko bread crumbs, and parsley in a medium bowl, and sprinkle over the pasta. Bake for 20 minutes, or until golden brown.

Yields 4 servings

Emperor's Tempura

*I*f you're anything like us, you'll be nibbling on these while you're cooking—that's how tempting these lightly batter-fried tempura vegetables are. And if there are any left over for dinner, serve them with rice and a salad.

DIPPING SAUCE

2 tablespoons soy sauce

1 tablespoon white or rice wine vinegar

1 tablespoon water

Freshly ground black pepper

TEMPURA VEGETABLES

1 quart canola oil, for frying

2 cups all-purpose flour

1 cup soy milk

¾ cup water

1 teaspoon garlic powder

½ teaspoon freshly ground black pepper

Broccoli florets (from about 1 head)

1 russet potato, thinly sliced

1 sweet potato, peeled and thinly sliced

1 green squash, thinly sliced

Whisk together all of the ingredients for the dipping sauce. Set aside.

In a 2-quart pot over medium-high, heat the canola oil to 325°F.

To make the batter, mix together the flour, soy milk, water, garlic powder, and pepper in a bowl.

Dip the sliced veggies into the batter. Drop the broccoli and squash into the heated oil, being careful not to crowd the pot. The veggies will sink to the bottom, then rise. Once the have risen, fry them for 2 to 3 minutes, then remove them to a wire rack set over a baking sheet. Repeat this step with the sweet potato and potato slices, frying them for 3 to 4 minutes.

Yields about 55 pieces

Rainbow Pasta

Sweet and savory, this pasta boasts red grapes, black olives, tomatoes, and romaine—a light, lovely pasta perfect for a summer day. Whenever we set down this plate of goodness in front of Justin, life feels right. It's perfect warm or at room temperature.

8 ounces penne pasta

½ cup red grapes, halved

6 large pitted black olives, sliced

4 plum tomatoes, diced

3 cups sliced romaine lettuce

2 tablespoons olive oil

2 tablespoons soy butter

1 tablespoon soy sauce

Freshly ground black pepper

½ cup shredded vegan mozzarella cheese

Cook the pasta in a large pot of boiling water according to the package directions, until al dente.

Put the red grapes, olives, tomatoes, and romaine into a large bowl. Drain the pasta and pour over the grapes and veggies in the bowl. Mix in the olive oil, soy butter, soy sauce, and pepper. Add the vegan mozzarella cheese and toss. Serve warm or at room temperature.

Yields 4 servings

Herbed Grilled "Cheeze" Sandwich in Basil Oil

This sandwich can certainly be made with store-bought bread and grilled with soy butter or olive oil, but an old-fashioned grilled cheese sandwich is taken to new heights here with homemade wheat bread and basil-infused olive oil. Time-consuming, but worth every minute.

True story: Justin actually stared at this sandwich for a good five minutes before he would eat it. Even at thirteen, the green olive oil took him aback. But before the sandwich went cold . . . he took a whiff . . . he nodded tentatively . . . he took that first bite, and stated, for the record: "Awesome, Mom!"

HEARTY HOMEMADE WHEAT BREAD
(YIELDS 2 LOAVES)

2 cups warm water
3 teaspoons active dry yeast
½ cup honey

3⅓ cups bread flour
3 tablespoons soy butter, melted

2 teaspoons kosher salt	1¾ cups whole wheat flour, plus more for flouring surface
	1 tablespoon olive oil

Grease two 9 × 5-inch loaf pans.

In a large bowl, mix together the warm water, yeast, and ¼ cup of the honey. Add the bread flour, and stir to combine. Let set for 45 minutes.

Mix in 2 tablespoons of the melted soy butter, the remaining ¼ cup honey, and salt. Stir in 1 cup of the whole wheat flour. Flour a flat surface and knead with approximately ¾ cup whole wheat flour until just sticky to the touch. Place in a large flour-dusted bowl and pour the olive oil over the dough, making sure the entire surface of the dough is coated. Cover with a dish towel and allow to rise until the dough has doubled in volume, about 45 minutes. Punch down the dough, and divide into 2 loaves. Place the dough into the prepared loaf pans, and allow to rise until the dough has nearly reached the rim of the pans, about 2 hours.

Preheat the oven to 350°F. Bake the loaves for 25 to 30 minutes, making sure not to overbake. Lightly brush the tops of the baked loaves with the remaining 1 table-spoon melted soy butter. Set aside to cool.

BASIL OLIVE OIL
(YIELDS APPROXIMATELY 1 CUP)

1½ cups (packed)
fresh basil leaves
(no stems)

¾ cups olive oil

Sea salt

Freshly ground black
pepper

Blanch the basil in boiling water for 1 second. Plunge into ice water for 5 seconds. Pat dry with paper towels. Combine the basil and olive oil in a blender or food processor and pulse until puréed. Season with salt and pepper to taste. Use immediately or store in the refrigerator for up to 2 weeks.

ASSEMBLY (FOR 1 SANDWICH)

Spread the basil oil on two thick slabs of herbed wheat bread. Add a generous amount of vegan cheddar cheese between the two slabs of bread. Place in a skillet over medium-heat and cook on each side for about 3 minutes, or until golden brown.

Variation: Add bacon strips, tomato slices, and/or thinly sliced Vidalia or Spanish onion to accent this sandwich. The basil oil also makes a wonderful topping for warm veggies, potatoes, rice, and pasta.

Grandma's Bulgogi

When it comes to Korean cooking, we bow to our mom. And once Justin's taste buds came of age, some sophisticated flavors were in order. Korean food often incorporates sesame oil and sesame seeds, but as long as garlic, ginger, scallions, and soy sauce are in the mix, sesame isn't really missed in this national dish of Korea.

Traditionally, bulgogi is served with rice but the younger Korean generation also wraps up these marinated beef strips in romaine leaves or soft tacos (check ingredients for possible allergens).

1 pound beef tenderloin, sliced paper thin against the grain into 3-inch lengths

1 bunch scallions, split lengthwise and cut into 1-inch sections

⅓ cup soy sauce

⅓ cup water

¼ cup sugar

3 garlic cloves, minced

2 teaspoons peeled and minced fresh ginger

¼ cup red wine

Combine all of the ingredients in a medium bowl and mix thoroughly. Cover with plastic wrap and place in the refrigerator to marinate for 3 hours or overnight; the longer you marinate, the more tender the beef will be.

Remove the beef from the refrigerator and bring to room temperature, about 1 hour before cooking. Fire up the grill pan or grill. Remove the beef and scallions from the marinade, spread out, and cook until caramelized.

Yields 4 servings

Hot and Bubbly Lasagna

Oozing with two kinds of "cheese" and lean ground beef, this version of lasagna would make Pavarotti sing, especially if he suffered from allergies. Nutritious, delicious, and satisfying, this lasagna is so good Justin has to share it with the rest of us. He's a generous boy, as long as there are leftovers. He likes to come home from school and cut up a little lasagna cube for a snack before diving into homework. Instant energy!

1 tablespoon olive oil

1 medium onion, diced

2 plum tomatoes, chopped

2 garlic cloves, minced

1 pound ground beef

One 15-ounce can tomato sauce

5 fresh basil leaves, chopped

1 tablespoon sugar

12 ounces firm tofu, mashed

16 ounces vegan mozzarella cheese, shredded, plus 4 ounces vegan mozzarella cheese, shredded

8 ounces vegan cheddar cheese, shredded

2 sprigs fresh parsley

Sea salt

Freshly ground black pepper

16 lasagna noodles

In a large skillet over medium heat, warm the olive oil. And the chopped onion, tomatoes, and garlic and sauté until the onion is soft. Add the ground beef and cook until browned. Add the tomato sauce, basil, and sugar. Simmer for 30 minutes. In a bowl, combine the mashed tofu, the 16 ounces of vegan mozzarella cheese, of vegan cheddar cheese, and parsley. Season with salt and pepper to taste and mix well.

Preheat the oven to 375°F.

Bring a large pot of water to a boil. Cook the lasagna noodles for 8 to 10 minutes, or until al dente. Because the noodles will finish cooking in the oven, it's important not to overcook them.

Spread a layer of sauce in the bottom of a 9 × 13-inch baking dish. Arrange 4 noodles lengthwise over the sauce. Add a layer of the vegan cheese–tofu mixture. Repeat the layering three times. Sprinkle the 4 ounces of vegan mozzarella cheese on top of the final noodle layer. Cover the lasagna with aluminum foil that has been coated with nonstick cooking spray. Bake for 30 minutes. Remove the foil, and cook for

15 minutes more. Cool for 20 minutes before cutting and serving.

Yields 6 servings

Panko Chicken Tenders

Whenever the family goes on vacation, our mom gets these sudden hankerings for Popeyes Chicken. On more than one occasion, we've had to pull off the road so she can get her fix. While she munches away, the car fills up with the smell of deep-fried chicken and greasy paper towels. We find it somewhat nauseating, but whatever makes Grandma happy!

With this recipe, Justin can have his fix, too—and without all that grease. The Dijon mustard gives the chicken a nice zing.

By the way, Grandma now loves this chicken, too—more than she loves Popeyes!

3 boneless, skinless chicken breasts

¼ cup soy butter, melted

2 garlic cloves, minced

1 tablespoon soy sauce

¼ cup Dijon mustard

1 tablespoon vegan mayonnaise

½ cup dairy-free panko bread crumbs

½ cup shredded vegan mozzarella cheese

1 tablespoon dried parsley flakes

1 teaspoon freshly ground black pepper

Preheat the oven to 350°F. Coat a 9 × 11-inch pan with nonstick cooking spray.

Slice the chicken breasts into 3-inch strips about ½ inch thick. Set aside.

In a large bowl, mix the melted soy butter, garlic, soy sauce, mustard, and vegan mayo. Set aside.

In a medium bowl, mix the panko bread crumbs, vegan mozzarella cheese, parsley, and pepper. Set aside.

Coat the chicken pieces in the mustard sauce on both sides and roll in the panko mixture. Place in the prepared pan. Bake for 45 minutes.

Yields 4 servings

Justin was enjoying his last lazy summer days before the start of second grade. But not all was bliss—Ginger had to break the news to him.

"It's time for another allergy test," she said.

Justin handled the news like a brave little man. "OK."

Meanwhile, we'd been holding our breaths. Imagine if Justin could start a new school year allergy-free. Life would be such a breeze! No EpiPen at the school clinic, no "special" lunches to pack, no worries or fears.

This time, instead of the usual prick test, the doctor suggested a blood test called RAST, an allergen-specific IgE (immunoglobulin E) antibody blood test used to screen for an allergy to a specific food. If levels are high, then it's likely a person is allergic to that food. The RAST test is also an indicator of whether a person will outgrow their allergy (however, not the severity of the reaction).

While the prick test is invaluable, no test is foolproof, particularly in children with sensitive skin who suffer from eczema like Justin. But the RAST, the doctor indicated, would give us a more complete understanding of Justin's food allergies.

Justin was tested for his four main food culprits: milk protein, peanuts, eggs, and sesame. We had to wait a week before the results came back, and what a long week it was, with us praying for good results, even just a sign that he was outgrowing his allergies, or even just one allergy.

Alas, the test results revealed that Justin was still highly allergic to all of the foods tested. The doctor advised us to come back in a year.

MOUTHWATERING TREATS

Whenever we have company over, we serve the treats in this section—it's important Justin knows he can dig in, too. Of course, we always make extra So-Good Scones for Grandma, who can never resist a scone, especially one chock-full of blueberries. Justin's favorites, however, are the Brown-Bag Brownies. And without exception, our friends love them too. We hear the same sentiment over and over: "You should sell these in your shop!" Well, currently we sell only chocolate and candies, but you never know.

Choco-Banana Bread

When Justin was in elementary school, packing goodies for his snack time and lunch periods wasn't as simple as tossing Twinkies or granola bars into his lunch box. Indeed, while at Safeway checking out the ingredients in baked goods such as Entenmann's, we'd often lamented that there wasn't a single thing on the shelves Justin could eat. With an allergic kid, every crumb counts, for even a minute amount of butter or whey can land the child in the emergency room.

Wanting a yummy yet energizing and wholesome snack, the notion of banana bread seemed feasible, and after a few misses, we worked it out. Banana bread is often walnut-studded but since nuts weren't on Justin's menu, we added chocolate chips for an irresistible treat that gave him plenty of bragging rights at school.

3 medium or 2 large ripe
 bananas
1½ cups all-purpose flour
½ cup sugar
¼ cup soy butter, softened
1 teaspoon pure vanilla
 extract

1 teaspoon baking soda
½ teaspoon baking powder
¼ cup unsweetened apple-
 sauce
½ cup dairy-free semisweet
 chocolate chips

Preheat the oven to 350°F. Grease and lightly flour a 9 × 5-inch loaf pan.

In a large bowl, mash up the bananas with a fork. Add the remaining ingredients, except for the chocolate chips, and mix together. Stir in the chocolate chips. Pour the batter into the prepared loaf pan. Bake for 45 to 55 minutes.

Yields one 9 × 5-inch loaf

Hot Milky Chocolate and Hot Mo' Chocolate

Our traditional recipe is perfect for Justin's dad Skip, who grew up on Swiss Miss and loves his hot chocolate milky. Justin, on the other hand, got his genes from us, his mom and aunt, the Chocolate Queens—he's the King of Chocolate! Both recipes are simple and satisfying—it's just a matter of more or less chocolate chips.

3 cups vanilla soy milk
½ teaspoon ground cinnamon
1 teaspoon pure vanilla extract

Dairy-free semisweet chocolate chips:
1 cup for Hot Milky Chocolate
1½ cups for Hot Mo' Chocolate

Heat up the soy milk. Stir in the cinnamon and vanilla. Stir in the chocolate chips.

Top with mini marshmallows or dunk our Chocolate Chocolate Chip Cookies (page 148) into the hot chocolate for a totally chocolate dripping experience.

Yields 3 servings

French Puffs

Francie's a fantastic assistant in the kitchen. And even though she's religiously watched certain cooking shows for years and has memorized many chefs' techniques, and even though she's spent many an hour in the kitchen with Ginger helping to perfect recipes and can tell what works and what doesn't, there's one undisputed reality: Baking's not her forte.

When Francie was in the eighth grade, each student in her French class was asked to prepare and bring a French dish to school. She decided to attempt French Puffs (mini muffins topped with a cinnamon-sugar-butter glaze). She followed a recipe she found, most likely from the only source we owned in those days, a Betty Crocker cookbook, hoping to turn out sweet, airy puffs of pastry. Instead, her "delicacies" came out of the oven looking like hockey pucks, each one heavy enough to use as a doorstop. Not wanting to be graded poorly for not turning in a dish, she brought them to class and to this day is eternally grateful to a girl named Karen who actually thought they tasted good and ate them all. Our French Puffs are light and airy, a far cry from Francie's "treats" of yore. And if her classmate Karen got the chance to taste our modern-day French Puffs, she would probably exclaim, *"Mon Dieu!"*

PUFFS

1½ cups all-purpose flour
½ cup sugar
1½ teaspoons baking powder
½ teaspoon sea salt
¼ cup unsweetened applesauce
½ cup soy milk
⅓ cup melted soy butter

TOPPING

⅓ cup melted soy butter
⅓ cup sugar mixed with 1½ teaspoons ground cinnamon

Preheat the oven to 350°F. Coat two mini muffin pans with nonstick cooking spray.

In a medium bowl, combine the flour, sugar, baking powder, and salt. In a separate medium bowl, combine the applesauce, soy milk, and soy butter. Pour the liquid ingredients into the dry ingredients and stir until incorporated. Do not overmix.

Fill the prepared muffin pans with batter. Bake for 15 to 20 minutes; the puffs will not turn golden. While still warm, dip the top of each puff into the melted butter and roll into the sugar-cinnamon mixture.

Yields 24 mini puffs

Brown-Bag Brownies

One day in the fourth grade, Justin came home from school a bit glum—it's a look every parent of an allergic child recognizes, the look of being left out because he or she couldn't eat the treat everyone else was eating. Here, a classmate had brought birthday brownies to share with everyone and, naturally, Justin couldn't have one. The next day, Ginger surprised him with a brownie in his lunch box that made him the envy of all his classmates. For the rest of that school year, whenever his friends came over, you could find them sniffing around the kitchen, hoping to find a fresh batch of Brown-Bag Brownies.

2 cups all-purpose flour
2 cups sugar
¾ cup unsweetened cocoa powder
1 teaspoon baking powder
1 teaspoon sea salt
2 tablespoons cornstarch

1 cup plus 2 tablespoons water
1 cup canola oil or 1 cup soy butter
1 teaspoon pure vanilla extract
⅔ cup dairy-free semisweet chocolate chips
Confectioners' sugar

Preheat the oven to 350°F. Grease and lightly flour a 13 × 9 × 2-inch glass baking dish.

In a large bowl, combine the flour, sugar, cocoa, baking powder, salt, and cornstarch. Add the water, oil or soy butter, and vanilla, and stir well. Add the chocolate chips. Pour the mixture into the prepared glass baking dish. Bake for 25 to 30 minutes. Remove from the oven and let cool. Refrigerate for 2 hours before cutting into squares of the desired size. Dust with confectioners' sugar.

Yields 12 to 15 brownies

Variation: Chocolate chips make these brownies gooey-good, but if you prefer more cake-like brownies, you can omit the chips.

Brown-Bag Blondies

One day not long ago, Ginger surprised her son with a blondie instead of a brownie. Famous chocoholic that she is, she had tossed in a heavy-handed dose of chocolate chips in this first test batch. After a few chews, Justin paused.

"So you said these are called 'blondies,' right, Mom?"

"Right—don't you like them?"

"Yeah, but I think you've got too many chocolate chips in here."

Sigh. In her second batch, Ginger lightened up on the chocolate chips. Fortunately, this recipe met with five-star approval. Yay!

1 cup all-purpose flour, plus flour for dusting the pan

½ cup soy butter, melted

1 cup packed light brown sugar

2 tablespoons unsweetened applesauce

1 tablespoon cornstarch

1 tablespoon water

1 teaspoon pure vanilla extract

¼ teaspoon baking soda

1 teaspoon baking powder

¼ teaspoon sea salt

⅓ cup dairy-free semisweet chocolate chips

Preheat the oven to 350°F. Grease and lightly flour an 8-inch square pan.

In a medium bowl, whisk together the melted butter and sugar. Add the applesauce, cornstarch, water, and vanilla and continue to whisk. Add the 1 cup flour, baking soda, baking powder, and salt and stir well. Mix in the chocolate chips.

Pour the mixture into the pan and spread it out evenly. Bake for 20 to 25 minutes. Remove from the oven and let cool. Cut into squares of the desired size.

Yields 9 to 12 blondies

Heavenly Cinnamon Buns

One afternoon, in the local mall, we passed a fragrant Cinnabon stall. The just-glazed cinnamon buns made both of us break out in a chorus of murmurs. Not Justin, though. At nine, he was a big boy now with big-boy realities: if he couldn't have one, he wouldn't murmur for one, either.

"I'm kind of tired of shopping," Ginger said.

"I am, too," Justin agreed.

"Good. Let's go home and make cinnamon buns."

Recreating cinnamon buns for Justin turned out to be a cinch, right down to the swirly whirly glaze—Justin's job. Ours left us even more happy and light-headed than the ones in the mall ever could.

DOUGH

¾ cup soy milk

¼ cup soy butter

3¼ cups all-purpose flour

1 package or 2¼ teaspoons instant yeast

¼ cup granulated sugar

½ teaspoon sea salt

2 tablespoons cornstarch

¼ cup plus 2 tablespoons water

1 cup packed brown sugar

1 tablespoon ground cinnamon

½ cup soy butter, softened

½ cup raisins (optional)

GLAZE

1 cup confectioners' sugar   2 tablespoons soy milk

Heat the soy milk in a small saucepan until it bubbles; remove from the heat. Mix in the soy butter and stir until melted. Set aside to cool until lukewarm.

In a large bowl, combine 2¼ cups of the flour, the yeast, granulated sugar, salt, and cornstarch and mix well. Add the water and the soy milk–soy butter mixture and beat well. Add the remaining 1 cup flour, ½ cup at a time, stirring well after each addition. When the dough just holds together, turn it out onto a lightly floured surface and knead until smooth, about 5 minutes. Cover the dough with a clean, damp kitchen towel and set aside for 15 minutes.

In a small bowl, mix together the brown sugar, cinnamon, and the 1/2 cup softened soy butter. Roll out the dough into a 9 × 12-inch rectangle. Spread the dough with the soy butter–sugar mixture. Sprinkle with raisins, if using. Working from the long side, roll up the dough and pinch the seam to seal. Cut the roll into 12 equal-size rolls and place in a 9 × 11-inch baking pan. Cover with a towel and let rise until doubled, about 45 minutes.

Preheat the oven to 375°F. Bake the rolls for 20 minutes, or until golden brown. Do not overbake.

To make the glaze, combine the confectioners' sugar and soy milk and mix with a spoon. Drizzle over the cooled buns.

Yields 12 buns

Blueberry Thrill

Except for our mom, none of us are in the habit of eating a bowl of blueberries, but they can be awesome in baked goods. Often, only a blueberry will do. When Ginger makes her blueberry crumble dish, she's been known to sing the famous Fats Domino lyric, "I found my thrill on Blueberry Hill." Seriously!

DOUGH

3 cups all-purpose flour

1 teaspoon baking powder

¼ teaspoon salt

Zest of 1 lemon

1 cup sugar

1 cup soy butter, chilled

¼ cup unsweetened apple-sauce

FILLING

½ cup sugar

4 teaspoons cornstarch

Juice of 1 lemon

4 cups fresh blueberries

Preheat the oven to 375°F. Grease a 9 × 13-inch pan.

In a medium bowl, combine the flour and baking powder. Mix in the salt, zest, and sugar. Using a fork or pastry cutter, blend in the soy butter and applesauce. The dough will be crumbly. Place half of the dough mixture into the pan and pat down gently to form a crust.

To make the filling, in a medium bowl, mix together the sugar, cornstarch, and lemon juice. With a rubber spatula, gently stir in the blueberries. Pour the blueberry mixture evenly over the crust. Crumble the remaining dough mixture over the berry mixture.

Bake for 45 minutes, or until the top is slightly browned. Cool completely before cutting into squares of the desired size.

Yields 12 to 15 squares

So-Good Scones

*a*fter we picked Justin up from preschool, we stopped at Starbucks for a noontime coffee break. Though he had been to many Starbucks before, this time something in the display case caught his eye. Scones.

"Can I have one of those, Mommy?"

As a tot, Justin understood he wasn't supposed to eat anything at school except the snack his mother packed for him. But he didn't yet understand what food allergies were.

"I'm sorry, pumpkin, no."

Yes, it was heartbreaking, but we never showed it.

A decade later, we were in the bakery section of a Whole Foods grabbing the last item on our list—a dairy-free apple pie—when Justin noticed the wire racks of baked goods.

"What goes into a scone, Mom?"

"The usual suspects, honey."

He groaned. "Milk and butter."

"And sour cream," Francie added.

Ginger turned the cart around and led the way to the refrigerated section. "We're not done shopping, gang." She was determined to make Justin a scone, and that's how this recipe was born.

DOUGH

8 tablespoons soy butter, frozen

2 cups all-purpose flour

⅓ cup sugar

1 teaspoon baking powder

⅓ teaspoon baking soda

½ teaspoon sea salt

½ cup non-dairy sour cream

2 tablespoons cornstarch

2 tablespoons water

½ cup dairy-free semisweet chocolate chips

TOPPING

1 tablespoon ground cinnamon

1 tablespoon sugar

Preheat the oven to 400°F.

Chop the butter into small pieces and place into a food processor along with all of the ingredients except for the chocolate chips. Pulse until smooth. The dough will be very thick. Place in a medium bowl and stir in the chocolate chips. Turn the dough out onto a floured surface and shape into an 8-inch circle about ¾ inch thick. Sprinkle with the cinnamon-sugar mixture. Cut into 8 even triangles. Place on an ungreased cookie sheet and bake for 15 to 20 minutes. Cool slighty before serving.

Yields 12 scones

Variation: To make cranberry-orange scones, substitute a ½ cup of dried cranberries for the chocolate chips and add 1 tablespoon of freshly squeezed orange juice and 1 teaspoon of orange zest. For blueberry scones, substitute 1 cup of fresh or frozen blueberries for the chocolate chips.

Where on Earth Is Justin's Cinnamon-Raisin Bagel?

*I*n 2001, our children's book *Where on Earth Is My Bagel?* was published. Our whimsical story about a Korean boy's craving for a New York bagel appealed to our youngest readers, including Justin. He loved the cinnamon-raisin bagels from the bagel shop up the street, but after one particular visit when he was five, he broke out in scary saucer-like hives; likely cross contamination, as the shop sold sesame bagels as well. Refusing to take any more chances, we decided homemade bagels were in order.

Chewy and dense, these freeze wonderfully for whenever Justin—like the character in our book—has a bagel craving.

4½ cups all-purpose flour

4½ teaspoons or 2 packages active dry yeast

1½ cups warm water

¼ cup sugar

1 teaspoon sea salt

1 tablespoon ground cinnamon

⅔ cup raisins

1 tablespoon sugar, for boiling water

Line two baking sheets with aluminum foil or parchment paper.

In the bowl of a stand mixer, combine 1½ cups of the flour with the yeast. In a medium bowl, combine the warm water with the sugar and salt. Add the liquid mixture to the flour mixture.

Place the bowl on the mixer and attach the dough hook. Mix on low speed for 1 minute, scraping down the sides of the bowl. Increase the speed to high and mix for 3 minutes. Stir in the remaining flour and the cinnamon and raisins. The dough should be stiff. (A handheld electric mixer can also be used: Mix on low speed for 1 minute; then mix on medium-high, slowly adding in the remaining flour and the cinnamon and raisins. Once combined, mix for 2 minutes more.)

Turn the dough out onto a lightly floured board and knead for about 3 minutes, or until the dough is smooth. Cover with a clean towel and let the dough rest for 15 minutes.

Preheat the oven to 375°F.

Roll the dough out into a log and twist off 12 even sections. Shape each section into a ball. Poke a finger through each ball and place on the lined baking sheets. Let rise another 15 minutes.

Meanwhile, bring a large pot of water with the 1 tablespoon of sugar to a boil. Reduce the heat to a simmer and drop 3 bagels at a time into the water. Cook for 5 to 7 minutes, flipping the bagels once. Remove the bagels using a flat spatula with holes, or a pair of tongs, and transfer them to paper towels to dry.

Place the bagels on the lined baking sheets and bake for 25 to 30 minutes until golden brown.

Yields 12 bagels

Variation: Try other wonderful variations such as substituting cinnamon and raisins with 2/3 cup of frozen blueberries or cranberries. If you're a savory soul, onion bagels are an easy choice: just increase the salt to 2 teaspoons, and add 1/2 cup of dehydrated onions and 1 teaspoon dried dill weed.

Spicy Savory Crackers

*D*ealing with a peanut allergy is challenging enough, but most people have no idea how all-encompassing a dairy allergy is. Before Justin was born, neither did we. A dairy-free diet? Just avoid milk, ice cream, cheese—the obvious culprits. But we soon learned that milk protein, also known as whey, casein, or caseinate, is listed on more ingredient labels than you can imagine, including most commercial cookies and crackers. We, the frustrated trio, have gone down many a grocery aisle on a mission to find assorted crackers for allergy sufferers, only to give up with a big fat sigh. Yes, there are water crackers; yes, there are some dairy-free varieties of Saltines—but come on! Isn't variety the spice of life?

Ginger decided that if she was going to make crackers, they would be very special crackers. And these are. Mission accomplished!

½ cup soy butter, at room
temperature

⅔ cup shredded
vegan mozzarella
cheese

⅔ cup shredded
vegan pepper
Jack cheese

1 teaspoon minced fresh
thyme leaves

½ teaspoon kosher salt

½ teaspoon garlic powder

½ teaspoon freshly ground
black pepper

1¼ cups all-purpose flour

Using an electric mixer, cream the soy butter. Add the vegan cheeses, thyme, salt, garlic salt, and pepper and mix on low speed until combined. Add the flour and continue to mix on low until the mixture is in large crumbles, about 1 minute. If the dough is too dry, add 1 or 2 teaspoons of water.

Place the dough onto a floured board, press into a ball, and roll into a 9-inch log. Wrap the log in plastic wrap and refrigerate for 1 hour.

Preheat the oven to 350°F. Line a baking sheet with parchment paper.

Cut the chilled log into ¼-inch rounds with a small, sharp knife and place them on the lined baking sheet. Bake for 25 minutes, or until very lightly browned, rotating the pan once, halfway through baking time. Cool and serve at room temperature. They can also be stored in an airtight container.

Yields 2 dozen crackers

Two Smoothies

The smoothie sky is the limit with key ingredients including soy milk, fruit, and crushed ice. These are Justin's favorites, but use our two examples as templates to create your own rich, luscious concoctions! We use lemon sorbet for one of our smoothies, but any sorbet flavor works wonders!

Choco-Banana Smoothie

½ cup vanilla soy milk

1 cup chocolate soy ice cream

1 medium banana

½ cup crushed ice

1 tablespoon chocolate syrup (check ingredients for possible allergens)

Place all of the ingredients in a blender and pulse until smooth. Serve chilled.

Yields 3 servings

Lemon-Banana Smoothie

½ cup vanilla soy milk   1 medium banana
½ cup vanilla soy ice cream   ½ cup crushed ice
½ cup lemon sorbet

Place all of the ingredients in a blender and pulse until
smooth. Serve chilled.

Yields 3 servings

ALLERGY REPORT 2008
AGE: TEN

We didn't go back to the allergist the next year, or even the next two years. It was almost easier to accept and cope with Justin's allergies than to get our hopes up every year only to be knocked down with the usual disappointing news. In fact, we were growing comfortable with our lifestyles, creating more recipes than we ever thought possible. Who needed to dine out? Who needed milk or eggs? Instead of making our own meals, we often ate what Justin ate; after all, they were tasty, healthy, and it made him happy to share.

One incident would forever change Francie's *que sera sera* attitude. It was when Justin innocently asked her a question: "What am I going to eat when I'm away at college?"

Francie had wondered about that—indeed, she and Ginger had already researched to see which colleges would accommodate his needs—but the fact that Justin was already worrying saddened her. Although he never showed it, maybe all the special preparations we took before going on picnics, day trips, and vacations had affected him more than we thought. Maybe he was sensitive to more than food.

"You don't worry about that, Justin, we'll figure everything out," Francie replied. After all, college was eight years away. "Besides, you're going to outgrow your food allergies before you go to college."

"I will?"

She decided right then and there that he would. It was as simple as that. And maybe if Justin believed it, too, that would double his chances. In a past generation, it might be called "The Power of Positive Thinking."

"Yes," she promised him.

Still, Justin's concern prompted us to make another appointment with the allergist. A new allergist. Not that there was anything wrong with our previous allergist, but he wasn't the most progressive doctor, and intuition told us it was time to move on. We found another doctor who was nice, but, in the end, we were left with the same message: You have an allergic child, period. She performed the usual prick test and sure enough, the results were unchanged from three years ago.

Still, Francie remained convinced that, maybe not today or tomorrow, but someday Justin would be allergy-free.

YAY COOKIES AND MUFFINS

When we were growing up, our family would visit Korea every three summers. This was in the '60s and '70s, still the postwar era. As kids, we didn't understand the poverty and disease in a place where nearly everyone dressed in rags. But even among the rubble we'd happen upon the occasional bakery shop called a ppang jip, or "Bread House," and our mom would lead us inside. The smell of freshly baked goods went up our noses and we sighed, so happy to be surrounded by heavenly treats. Sometimes when we are baking our Drop Sugar Cookies or Round-the-Clock "Milk" Muffins, aromas fill the kitchen and we fondly remember the ppang jips of yore.

Cookies Galore

When Justin was in the first grade, Francie attended a school tea where his classmates were unabashedly grabbing cookies, some homemade, some not, from the community tea cart. Meanwhile, she noticed Justin hiding the cookies she had packed up for him for this occasion. Store-bought, the treats were allergen-free and they looked exactly like the Oreos and Vienna Fingers on the tea cart. Still, Justin obviously felt ashamed. The sight of his little paws trying to cover his paper plate broke Francie's heart. Later that day, she relayed the story to her sister, who went into her cupboard and came out with a boxed cookie mix from a health food store. Most of Ginger's cooking time went into preparing wholesome meals—cookies had been on the back burner, so to speak.

"I've been meaning to make these," Ginger said, tying on her apron. "I just hope they're good."

Using non-dairy semisweet chocolate chips, chocolate chip cookies were possible. And out of the oven, they looked like the real thing. Francie tried one.

"Well," she said with a shrug, "it's no Toll House Chocolate Chip Cookie, that's for sure."

Ginger wasn't particularly impressed, either, but ultimately, Justin had never tasted a Toll House Chocolate Chip Cookie, and maybe it wasn't possible to mimic one in the kitchen or the ones on the tea cart. Like her son's persistent food allergies, maybe you just had to face up to some things: No butter or eggs = No flavor?

"How do these look, honey?" she asked, removing them from the foil-lined cookie sheet and placing them on a plate.

Justin was all smiles. "Good—can I have one?"

"That's why I made them, silly!"

He bit in. The taste of chocolate made him swoon, smile, and declare: "I love chocolate!" Then he gobbled the whole cookie down.

Success!

Or so we thought.

One day Justin had a friend over for a playdate.

Everything was fine until Ginger put out a plate of the chocolate chip cookies, fresh from the oven.

"That's the worst cookie in the world!" the friend cried, not knowing any better. He spit it out and threw it in the trash. "I don't know how you can eat those, Justin! My mother's cookies are a trillion times better!"

Lightning struck: It was time for Ginger to make her own cookies not from a box but from scratch and her own imagination. That innocent little incident changed her world. She had to think not in terms of just avoiding the allergen but also adding deliciously satisfying ingredients. The world was big; they were out there, somewhere. No matter what Paula Deen said, a person could live without butter.

That was eight years ago, and not only would Ginger's chocolate chip cookies become all the rage among Justin's friends, they'd blow away every cookie on that long-ago tea cart.

Justin's Favorite Chocolate Chip Cookies

*J*ustin loves all his mother's cookies, but this classic cookie is number one on his list. You'll always find a bag of these in Francie's freezer as well.

1 cup soy butter
½ cup sugar
1 cup packed brown sugar
1 teaspoon pure vanilla extract
2 tablespoons unsweetened applesauce

2 tablespoons cornstarch
2 tablespoons water
2½ cups all-purpose flour
1 teaspoon baking soda
1 teaspoon salt
2 cups dairy-free semisweet chocolate chips

Preheat the oven to 375°F.

In a large bowl, cream together the soy butter and sugars until smooth. Beat in the vanilla, applesauce, cornstarch, and water. Combine the flour, baking soda, and salt and stir into the sugar mixture. Mix in the chocolate chips.

Form the cookie dough into 1¼-inch balls. Place onto ungreased cookie sheets, 2 inches apart. Bake for 8 to 10 minutes until the edges are golden. Transfer from the cookie sheets to a wire rack to cool.

Yields about 24 cookies

Oatmeal-Raisin-Cranberry Cookies

We also call this "The Good Cookie." Moist and chewy, the oats and fruit make this little prize the perfect high-protein midmorning or afternoon snack. And one easily tucked into a lunch box.

1 cup soy butter

1 cup sugar

3 tablespoons water

3 tablespoons cornstarch

2 tablespoons unsweetened
    applesauce

2 cups all-purpose flour

2 cups old-fashioned oats

1 teaspoon baking powder

1 teaspoon baking soda

¼ teaspoon salt

1 teaspoon ground cinnamon

1 cup raisins

1 cup fresh cranberries,
    chopped

¼ cup soy milk

Preheat the oven to 350°F. Using an electric mixer, cream together the soy butter and sugar until light and fluffy. Add the water, cornstarch, and applesauce. Set the creamed ingredients aside.

In a separate large bowl, combine the remaining dry

ingredients, the raisins, and the cranberries. Add the dry ingredients to the creamed ingredients and stir to combine. Stir in the soy milk.

Drop heaping tablespoons of the cookie dough onto ungreased cookie sheets, 2 inches apart. Bake until golden brown and slightly crunchy, about 15 minutes. Transfer from the cookie sheets to a wire rack to cool.

Yields about 24 cookies

Chocolate Chocolate Chip Cookies

*g*uess what shop this cookie is named after? You can't get more chocolaty than this! We should know! After all, we come from a family of chocolate lovers. We were chocoholics before it was a word!

1 cup soy butter, softened

1½ cups sugar

2 teaspoons pure vanilla extract

3 tablespoons water

3 tablespoons cornstarch

2 tablespoons unsweetened applesauce

1½ cups all-purpose flour

½ cup cake flour

⅔ cup unsweetened cocoa powder

¾ teaspoon baking soda

¼ teaspoon sea salt

2 cups dairy-free semisweet chocolate chips

Preheat the oven to 350°F.

In a large bowl, beat the soy butter, sugar, and vanilla until light and fluffy. Mix in the water, cornstarch, and applesauce.

In a medium bowl, combine the flours, cocoa, baking soda, and salt; stir into the soy-butter mixture until well blended. Mix in the chocolate chips.

Form the cookie dough into 1¼-inch balls. Place onto ungreased cookie sheets, 2 inches apart. Bake for 8 to 10 minutes, or just until set. Transfer from the cookie sheets to a wire rack to cool.

Yields about 24 cookies

Shortbread Dipped into Dark Chocolate

These cookies made their debut in our family at Christmas 2009. Justin's uncle, aunts, and cousins were over and polished off every cookie on the platter—Justin was lucky to get one. And no wonder: They're beautiful, irresistible, and frankly there's just something about the experience of biting into a layer of chocolate over "buttery" shortbread that can't be beat.

1 cup soy butter, softened
½ cup confectioners' sugar
1 teaspoon pure vanilla
    extract

2 cups all-purpose flour
1½ cups dairy-free semisweet
    chocolate chips
4 teaspoons canola oil

Preheat the oven to 350°F.

In a medium bowl, using an electric mixer, cream the soy butter and confectioners' sugar. Add the vanilla. Gradually add the flour and mix well.

With lightly floured hands, form the cookie dough into 2 × 3/4-inch logs. Place the logs onto ungreased cookie sheets, 2 inches apart. Bake for 9 to 11 minutes until edges and bottom are lightly browned. Transfer from the cookie sheets to a wire rack to cool.

In a small microwave-safe bowl, melt the chocolate chips and canola oil together; stir until smooth. Dip half of each cookie into the chocolate, and set on wax or parchment paper until cool.

Yields about 24 shortbreads

Soy Nut Butter Cookies

Once upon a time, we used to bake cakes, cookies, and even tiny pizzas together in Ginger's Easy-Bake Oven. Years later, Ginger would move on into the real kitchen. And of course, in "Cookies 101," whipping up a batch of Peanut Butter Cookies is one of the first lessons.

These days Ginger can barely remember ever opening a jar of peanut butter. Does she miss it? No way! Soy nut butter is a wonderful substitute.

1½ cups all-purpose flour
¼ cup cake flour
¾ teaspoon baking soda
¾ teaspoon sea salt
1¼ cups packed brown sugar
¾ cup soy nut butter

½ cup shortening, preferably non-hydrogenated
3 tablespoons vanilla soy milk
1 tablespoon pure vanilla extract
2 tablespoons cornstarch
2 tablespoons water

Preheat the oven to 375°F.

In a medium bowl, combine the flours, baking soda, and salt. Set aside.

In a medium bowl, combine the sugar, soy nut butter, shortening, vanilla soy milk, and vanilla. Using an electric mixer, mix on low speed until blended. Add the cornstarch and water and mix until blended, being careful not to overbeat. Add the dry ingredients and mix just until blended.

Form the dough into 1½-inch balls and place onto ungreased cookie sheets, 2 inches apart. Using the back of a fork, press a crisscross decoration on the top of each cookie. Bake for 10 to 12 minutes. Transfer from the cookie sheets to a wire rack to cool.

Yields about 36 cookies

Lemon Cornmeal Cookies

When a cookie has this much character, you know it's yummy. Our Lemon Cornmeal Cookie is hearty, not too sweet, and full of texture. "Chew-licious!"

1 cup all-purpose flour
⅓ cup yellow cornmeal
½ teaspoon baking soda
¼ teaspoon sea salt
¼ teaspoon ground ginger
¾ cup sugar

6 tablespoons soy butter
1 tablespoon cornstarch
2 tablespoons unsweetened applesauce
1 tablespoon water
1 tablespoon grated lemon zest

Preheat the oven to 350°F.

In a medium bowl, combine the flour, cornmeal, baking soda, salt, and ginger and mix thoroughly.

In a large mixing bowl, combine the sugar and soy butter. Using an electric mixer, beat at medium speed until light and fluffy, 3 to 5 minutes. Beat in the cornstarch, applesauce, and water. Beat in the lemon zest.

Add the flour mixture to the sugar-butter mixture, and beat on medium-low speed just until blended.

Spoon the batter by tablespoonsful onto ungreased cookie sheets, 2 inches apart. Bake for 10 to 12 minutes until lightly browned. Transfer from the cookie sheets to a wire rack to cool.

Yields about 12 cookies

Drop Sugar Cookies

In the old days, our mom—who did not grow up eating Christmas cookies—had found two recipes for holiday cookies. Her first attempt was a no-name cookie and it was made with drained canned fruit. Yuck! The other was a drop sugar cookie that she would sprinkle with glittery red or green sugar. Yum! For our dad, who preferred his sugar cookies crispy and a bit browned, she would leave a small batch in the oven for an extra minute or so.

But why just enjoy them at Christmas? We bake our Drop Sugar Cookies year-round and they can be whipped up with a few key ingredients. Justin likes them soft and a bit chewy while Francie, like our dad, has grown to prefer them thin and a bit crispy—we simply leave them in the oven a little longer for her.

¾ cup confectioners' sugar
½ cup granulated sugar
½ cup vegetable oil

½ cup soy butter
1 teaspoon pure vanilla extract

1 tablespoon cornstarch
1 tablespoon water
2 tablespoons unsweetened
   applesauce

2¼ cups all-purpose flour
½ teaspoon baking soda
½ teaspoon cream of tartar

Preheat the oven to 350°F.

In a medium bowl, using an electric mixer, cream together the sugars, oil, and soy butter. Cream in the vanilla, cornstarch, water, and applesauce. Add the flour, baking soda, and cream of tartar to the creamed mixture.

Roll the dough into 1-inch balls. Roll one side of each ball into sugar and place onto ungreased cookie sheets, 2 inches apart. Bake for 10 to 12 minutes. Transfer from the cookie sheets to a wire rack to cool.

Yields about 36 cookies

Muffin Mayhem

Muffins are a friendly food with their funny mushroom tops and crumbly nature. They're also a pinch to make, yummy to eat, and freeze beautifully.

Round-the-Clock "Milk" Muffins

Justin enjoys snacking on these muffins at any hour, hence the name. Sometimes he'll grab one for breakfast, or pack a few in his tennis bag. Now that he's in high school, he stays up later on weekends, and you can imagine what he's munching on while he's watching the shows he missed during the week. He prefers his Round-the-Clock "Milk" Muffins plain, but they're awfully good with a pat o' soy butter or a little jam, too.

3 cups all-purpose flour
1 cup sugar
4 teaspoons baking powder
½ teaspoon sea salt
½ cup unsweetened apple-sauce
1 cup soy milk
½ cup canola oil

Preheat the oven to 400°F. Coat a 12-well muffin pan with nonstick cooking spray, or line with paper cups.

In a large bowl, combine the dry ingredients. Set aside. In a medium bowl, combine the wet ingredients and whisk to incorporate. Pour the wet ingredients into the bowl of dry ingredients and mix with a spoon.

Fill the prepared muffin pan. Bake for 18 to 20 minutes until the muffins are golden on top.

Yields 12 muffins

Raisin-Apricot Bran Muffins

Packed with bran and jewels of dried fruit, these moist muffins are nutritious on-the-go treats—not to mention a great way to sneak some fiber into your child's diet.

1¼ cups all-purpose flour
¼ cup granulated sugar
¼ cup lightly packed light brown sugar
1 tablespoon baking powder
¼ teaspoon sea salt
2 cups bran cereal

1¼ cups vanilla soy milk
¼ cup unsweetened apple-sauce
¼ cup vegetable oil
15 small dried apricots, diced
⅔ cup raisins

Preheat the oven to 400°F. Coat a 12-well muffin pan with nonstick cooking spray, or line with paper cups.

In a medium bowl, combine the flour, sugars, baking powder, and salt. Set the dry ingredients aside.

In a large bowl, combine the bran cereal and soy milk. Let stand for 4 minutes to soften the cereal. Add the applesauce and oil and beat well. The bran will not break apart, and the batter will not be smooth.

Add the dry ingredients along with the apricots and raisins to the wet ingredients and stir with a large spoon until combined.

Fill the prepared muffin pan. Bake for 18 to 20 minutes until the muffins are golden on top.

Yields 12 muffins

Lemon Zest "Sour Cream" Muffins

In our day, long before video games and the Internet, summer was all about the great outdoors: roller skating and playing tag, running through the sprinkler, and setting up lemonade stands to make a few bucks. It was like seeing a blast from the past when one hot summer day Justin and his friend were feeling entrepreneurial and decided to open a lemonade stand in the neighborhood. The ingredients couldn't be simpler: lemons, sugar, water, ice. In the kitchen, Ginger took a sip and gave it her thumbs-up. "Try it, Justin, it's pretty good."

He shrugged.

Even if Justin knows he can eat something new, he's always hesitant to try it the first time. That comes from years of being conscious of being allergic and, naturally, the fear of a reaction.

"You can drink the lemonade," Ginger assured him.

He took a tiny sip. Smile. "Hmm . . . I love lemons!"

Thus was the inspiration for this lemony muffin. And as a side note, Justin and his friend ended up with a pretty profitable day. Unlike us at Chocolate Chocolate, however, they didn't open up shop the next morning.

MUFFINS

2 cups all-purpose flour

⅔ cup sugar

2 teaspoons baking powder

¼ teaspoon baking soda

¼ teaspoon salt

2 tablespoons cornstarch

2 tablespoons water

Zest and juice of 1 lemon

¾ cup non-dairy sour cream

¼ cup unsweetened applesauce

1 teaspoon pure vanilla extract

¼ cup lemon extract

1 cup soy butter, melted

GLAZE

1 cup confectioners' sugar

1 tablespoon freshly squeezed lemon juice

Preheat the oven to 375°F. Coat a 12-well muffin pan with nonstick cooking spray, or line with paper cups.

In a medium bowl, combine the dry ingredients, including the lemon zest. Set aside.

Put the wet ingredients into a separate medium

bowl and whisk to combine. Pour the wet ingredients over the dry ingredients and mix with a large spoon. Be careful not to overmix; the batter should be lumpy.

Fill the prepared muffin pan. Bake for 15 to 20 minutes until the muffins are golden on top.

To make the glaze, combine the confectioners' sugar and lemon juice in a bowl. Stir with a spoon until smooth. Drizzle over the cooled muffins.

Yields 12 muffins

Choco-Orange Muffins

 Every day at our shop we are asked, "Do you have chocolate with orange in it?" It's a terrific combo that works in both bonbons and muffins.

½ cup soy butter
1 cup sugar
¼ cup unsweetened apple-
  sauce
½ cup non-dairy sour cream
½ cup freshly squeezed
  orange juice
2 tablespoons water

2 tablespoons grated orange
  zest
2 cups all-purpose flour
2 tablespoons cornstarch
1 teaspoon baking powder
½ teaspoon baking soda
⅔ cup dairy-free semisweet
  chocolate chips

Preheat the oven to 400°F. Coat a 12-well muffin pan with nonstick cooking spray, or line with paper cups.

In a medium bowl, using an electric mixer, cream together the soy butter and sugar. Beat in the apple-sauce, non-dairy sour cream, orange juice, water, and orange zest.

In a large bowl, combine the flour, cornstarch, baking powder, baking soda, and chocolate chips. Using a spoon, stir the wet mixture into the dry mixture just until moistened.

Fill the prepared muffin pan. Bake for 15 to 20 minutes until the muffins are golden on top.

Yields 12 muffins

Oh-So-Sweet Corn Bread Muffins

*L*ike our Best Biscuits Ever, these are great with our White Bean Turkey Chili.

1 cup all-purpose flour
1 cup yellow cornmeal
¼ cup granulated sugar
¼ cup packed brown sugar
1 teaspoon sea salt
2 tablespoons cornstarch

3 teaspoons baking powder
1 cup vanilla soy milk
2 tablespoons water
¼ cup unsweetened apple-sauce
⅓ cup cold soy butter, cut into pieces

Preheat the oven to 400°F. Coat a 12-well muffin pan with nonstick cooking spray, or line with paper cups.

In a large bowl, combine the flour, cornmeal, sugars, salt, cornstarch, and baking powder. Stir in the soy milk, water, applesauce, and soy butter until well combined.

Fill the prepared muffin pan. Bake for 15 to 20 minutes until the muffins are golden on top.

Yields 12 muffins

Chocolate Breakfast Muffins

Not too sweet, and perfect with a tall glass of soy milk.

¼ cup unsweetened apple-sauce

½ cup canola oil

2 tablespoons water

1 cup soy milk

1 teaspoon pure vanilla extract

1¾ cups all-purpose flour

2 tablespoons cornstarch

½ cup sugar

⅔ cup unsweetened cocoa powder

1 tablespoon baking powder

½ teaspoon sea salt

⅔ cup dairy-free semisweet chocolate chips (plus extra chips for sprinkling on top)

Preheat the oven to 400°F. Coat a 12-well muffin pan with nonstick cooking spray, or line with paper cups.

In a large bowl, combine the applesauce, oil, water, soy milk, and vanilla. In a smaller bowl, combine the flour, cornstarch, sugar, cocoa, baking powder, salt, and chocolate chips. Combine wet and dry mixtures and fold together gently until just mixed.

Fill the prepared muffin pan and sprinkle the chocolate chips on top of each. Bake for 15 to 20 minutes until the muffins form a peak.

Yields 12 muffins

ALLERGY REPORT 2010
AGE: TWELVE

In the spring of 2010, we were scouring the Internet for allergy information when we stumbled upon a blog about a boy in Boston with a life-threatening dairy allergy who outgrew his allergy by consuming tiny amounts of milk each day in a controlled environment where doctors could monitor and save him from a possible anaphylactic reaction. By his next birthday, he was celebrating with pizza topped with REAL cheese. We'd heard of this technique before, but only in theory. Now here it was, right on our computer screen. Hope flooded our faces as we searched for more information.

Soon we came upon a video featuring a well-known doctor who spoke about the cutting-edge research being conducted at a university hospital. It mirrored the Boston boy's study. Excited, we decided to attend one of the doctor's seminars being held at a local library.

The seminar was just getting underway when we got there. Suddenly, we knew we weren't alone in the world; the statistics regarding the increasing number of allergic children were true: at least eighty parents were present. And many of their children, we realized, suffered more than Justin. One father spoke of his child who was allergic to dairy, tree nuts, legumes, eggs, gluten, and almost all fruits. One mother told us that her child was allergic to everything but chicken.

The latest study, the doctor explained, indicated that a good number of severely allergic children outgrow their food allergies by continuous exposure to the allergen in increasingly minute doses, thus supporting the Boston child's experience. The catch was that this treatment was still in the experimental stage. We left the seminar with a sense of promise. In the car on the way home, Francie said what she'd said so many times, with more conviction than ever: "Justin's going to outgrow his allergies. Period."

We sought out yet another new allergy group in the hopes that this office would embrace a more cutting-edge philosophy. We'd heard about "food challenges" for children whose allergy tests indicated a mild allergy. The challenge took place in the allergist's office—basically the patient is given the smallest dose of an allergen to test for a reaction. Unfortunately, the allergist Ginger and Skip met with was definitely old-school. After running skin prick tests and examining the results, he expressed his opinion: "Your son's allergies are so severe I wouldn't recommend a food challenge."

When Ginger called Francie with the latest allergy report, Francie was puzzled; in her heart of hearts, she was positive these results would reveal that Justin was outgrowing his allergies or, at the very least, that they were getting milder and that he was finally on the road to being allergy-free!

It was at this time she began "imaging" her nephew drinking milk—in the middle of the day, in the middle of the night, whenever she thought of it, which was often. Call it mind over matter or just the power of positive thinking, she continued creating these images in her head day after day, week after week, month after month. She'd already promised Justin that someday his results would come back differently, and she would make that happen, she promised herself.

A few months later, Justin was back in the allergist's office, this time for a flu shot, as his severe egg allergy required him to have his flu shot administered by an allergist. Even though Justin's allergy tests indicated he was allergic to eggs, he never reacted negatively to the flu shot.

The allergist that day was a young woman who was intently studying his chart while we gathered our things to leave.

"Wait a minute," she said, "the last time he had a RAST blood test was in 2005. Based on his non-reaction to eggs in the flu shot, I think it's time for another."

"But he just had skin prick tests a few months ago," Ginger said.

"Allergy testing isn't always a science. There are false positives, and that can be both frustrating and confusing. Plus, I see in his file that he suffers from eczema, which can interfere with a skin test result. I really think it's time for a RAST test."

More progressive than her colleague, this allergist was a breath of fresh air. Maybe even hopeful.

!!! DESSERTS

Our childhood friends were envious of our mom's exotic culinary ways in the kitchen. She would serve us galbi, Korean-style short ribs, ja ja mein—buckwheat noodles in a rich, dark sauce with tiny cubed potatoes, topped off with cucumber slivers and scallions—and omi rice, a mound of fried rice covered with a flat omelette so thin you could see through it. Our mom never took shortcuts; she was always cooking up a storm, and as long as she wasn't preparing Western food, we knew we were going to dine like royalty. Yet one thing was always missing—dessert. Even though she's a chocoholic, desserts just weren't on the Korean menu.

Our American friends always had desserts, though, and so would Justin.

How best to end a meal—and our cookbook—than with these sumptuous desserts? From our Golden Butter Cake to our Peach Cobbler to Justin's 5-Star Truffles, your child will always feel special in the sweetest way. And that is how it should be.

Applesauce Cake with Dream-Cheeze Glazing

When it comes to baking for children with egg allergies, applesauce is a godsend. It's also a fantastic way to sneak fruit into a diet. This cake had been a staple in Ginger's kitchen for years, but the minute non-dairy cream cheese became available on the market, she couldn't resist experimenting with a sweet glaze to finish off the cake. When Justin first tried it, he was admittedly nervous, especially now that he understood the serious nature of his allergies. But fear not. His eyes lit up like they did on his first birthday when he tasted vanilla ice cream cake—only this time, no hives.

Success!

CAKE

2 cups all-purpose flour, plus some for dusting the pan

⅔ cup soy butter

1 cup sugar

1 cup unsweetened apple-sauce

1 teaspoon baking soda

1 teaspoon ground cinnamon

¼ teaspoon ground nutmeg

2 tablespoons cornstarch

2 tablespoons water

1 cup raisins

GLAZE

8 ounces non-dairy cream cheese

⅓ cup soy butter

1 cup confectioners' sugar, sifted

1 teaspoon pure vanilla extract

Preheat the oven to 350°F. Grease and lightly flour an 8 × 8 × 2-inch cake pan.

In a medium bowl, using an electric mixer, cream together the butter and sugar. Add the applesauce and beat until smooth. Stir in the flour, baking soda, cinnamon, nutmeg, cornstarch, and water. Mix in the raisins.

Pour the batter into the prepared cake pan. Bake for 40 to 45 minutes. Set aside to cool.

To make the glaze, using an electric mixer, cream

together the non-dairy cream cheese and soy butter. Sift in the confectioners' sugar. Add the vanilla and whip until creamy. Glaze the cake while it is in the pan and then cut to serve.

Yields one 8-inch cake

A Birthday Cake for Justin

We made this cake for Justin's second birthday, and now a birthday isn't a birthday without this cake. One slice of this rich, moist, chocolate chip–studded cake is never enough. Though made without eggs or butter, amazingly this cake can stand up to any cake, even one from a fancy bakery box.

CAKE

3 cups all-purpose flour

2 cups sugar

½ cup unsweetened cocoa powder

2 teaspoons baking powder

2 teaspoons baking soda

⅔ cup canola oil

2 cups water

2 tablespoons distilled white vinegar

2 teaspoons pure vanilla extract

1 cup dairy-free semisweet chocolate chips

BUTTERCREAM ICING

½ cup vegetable shortening, preferably non-hydrogenated

½ cup soy butter, at room temperature

1 teaspoon pure vanilla extract

4 cups confectioners' sugar

2 tablespoons soy milk

Preheat the oven to 350°F. Coat two 9-inch round cake pans with nonstick cooking spray.

In a large bowl, combine all of the dry ingredients. Set aside. In a medium bowl, combine all of the wet ingredients. Pour the wet ingredients into the bowl of dry ingredients and beat until smooth.

Pour the batter into the prepared pans. The batter will be thinner than your usual cake batter. Fear not, this cake is rich and moist. Bake the cakes for about 30 minutes, or until a toothpick inserted in the middle comes out clean.

To make the buttercream icing, in a large bowl, using an electric mixer, cream together the shortening and soy butter. Beat in the vanilla. Add the sugar a cup at a time, beating it in well. Add the milk and beat until light and fluffy.

Once cakes are cooled, ice to your heart's content. Yields one 9-inch layer cake

Tip: Cut out parchment paper rounds, line the bottom of the cake pans, and lightly flour for easier release of the cakes.

Golden Butter Cake

Our mom is famously the original chocoholic in our family; however, she's also a pound cake freak. So for her birthday, she usually requests this "buttery" cake with chocolate icing. Having polished off her first bite, she's been known to exclaim, "I can't believe it's not butter!"

CAKE

1½ cups soy butter, softened

2 cups sugar

2 cups vanilla soy milk

2 teaspoons pure vanilla extract

1 cup soft tofu

4 cups cake flour

4 teaspoons baking powder

1 teaspoon sea salt

CHOCOLATE DECADENCE ICING

1 cup soy butter

1 teaspoon ground cinnamon

⅔ cup unsweetened cocoa powder

¼ cup vanilla soy milk

1 teaspoon pure vanilla extract

¼ teaspoon sea salt

2½ cups confectioners' sugar

Preheat the oven to 375°F. Coat two 9-inch round cake pans with nonstick cooking spray; cut out parchment paper rounds, line the bottom of the cake pans, and lightly flour for easier release of the cakes.

In a large bowl, using an electric mixer, cream together the soy butter and sugar until light and fluffy. Add the vanilla soy milk, vanilla, and tofu and mix until combined; the consistency will be a bit lumpy.

In a separate large bowl, combine the dry ingredients and mix thoroughly. Add the dry ingredients to the creamed mixture and, using an electric mixer, mix on low for 2 minutes. Increase the speed to high and beat for 2 minutes more, or until thick and creamy.

Pour the batter into the prepared cake pans. Bake the cakes for about 30 minutes or until a toothpick inserted in the center comes out clean.

To make the chocolate icing, in a large bowl, using an electric mixer, cream together the soy butter, cinnamon, and cocoa until smooth. Add the vanilla soy milk, vanilla, and salt and mix until thoroughly combined. Add the confectioners' sugar, 1/2 cup at a time, and mix in on low speed. Once all the sugar is combined, beat on high speed for 3 minutes more, or until light and creamy.

Once cakes are cooled, ice to your heart's content.

Yields one 9-inch round two-layer cake

Peach Cobbler

In the sixth grade, Justin began studying the Westward Expansion. Because our mom often tunes into old Westerns like *Wagon Train* and *The Virginian* (they take her back to her fondest days in this country), Justin was familiar with the cowboy eating experience—chewing on jerky, and eating beans off of tin plates.

But then one of the students' moms brought in an example of food from that period: a peach cobbler. Naturally, all of his classmates gobbled it up while Justin watched.

"She said she made it in a Dutch oven," he told his mom.

Hint, hint.

Our peach cobbler is made in a conventional oven, but is every bit as tempting as any made in a Dutch oven. Wonderful with soy ice cream or soy whipped cream.

PEACH FILLING

6 large ripe peaches, peeled, pitted, and cut into thin wedges

¼ cup granulated sugar

¼ cup packed brown sugar

½ teaspoon ground cinnamon

⅛ teaspoon ground nutmeg

1 teaspoon freshly squeezed lemon juice

2 teaspoons cornstarch

COBBLER BATTER

1 cup all-purpose flour

¼ cup granulated sugar

¼ cup packed brown sugar

1 teaspoon baking powder

½ teaspoon sea salt

6 tablespoons unsalted soy butter, chilled and cut into small pieces

¼ cup boiling water

TOPPING

1 teaspoon ground cinnamon 2 tablespoons white sugar

Preheat the oven to 425°F.

In a large bowl, combine the peaches, granulated sugar, brown sugar, cinnamon, nutmeg, lemon juice, and cornstarch. Mix well and pour into a 9 × 11-inch glass baking dish. Bake for 10 minutes.

Meanwhile, in another large bowl, make the batter. Combine the flour, granulated sugar, brown sugar, baking powder, and salt. Add the soy butter and mix with your hands until the mixture resembles coarse meal. Stir in the water until just combined.

Remove the peach filling from the oven and drop large spoonfuls of the batter over the peaches. Sprinkle the peach cobbler with the cinnamon-sugar topping. Bake the cobbler until golden brown, about 30 minutes.

Yields 10 to 12 servings

Deep Dark Chocolate Pudding

Even though Justin is in high school now, there are certain foods we remember feeding him for the first time, and this is one of them. Our memory: His anticipation at our sides while we prepared this pudding, his young face as the spoon went toward his lips, and the smile that followed. No disappointment here—a silky, velvety, chocolaty treat is part of what childhood is all about.

2 tablespoons cornstarch
½ cup sugar
¼ cup high-quality unsweetened cocoa powder
2½ cups soy milk

1 tablespoon soy butter
6 ounces semisweet chocolate (62% cocoa content), chopped
½ teaspoon pure vanilla extract

In a medium saucepan over medium heat, combine the cornstarch, sugar, and cocoa. Slowly whisk in approximately ½ cup of the milk and continue to whisk until smooth in texture. Slowly add the remaining milk, and cook, continuously whisking, until thick, about 3 minutes.

When the mixture has thickened, remove the pan from the heat. Slowly stir in the soy butter, chopped chocolate, and vanilla and mix until fully incorporated.

Divide the pudding among individual ramekins or serving bowls. Serve immediately or refrigerate, covered tightly with plastic wrap, until chilled.

Yields 4 servings

Apple-of-My-Eye Pie

When we discovered an all-natural dairy-free apple pie at the market, we were thrilled. We brought it home and sliced it up.

"Here, Justin!"

After a few bites, however, Justin seemed less than thrilled. Soon we understood why: Neither the crust nor the apples were completely cooked through. The next time we bought the pie, it was fine. Yet over time, the pie proved inconsistent; sometimes it was good, sometimes underbaked.

When you turn out your own pie, it's perfect every time!

APPLE PIE FILLING

½ cup soy butter

3 tablespoons all-purpose flour

¼ cup water

½ cup granulated sugar

½ cup lightly packed light brown sugar

½ teaspoon ground cinnamon

7 Granny Smith apples, peeled, cored, and sliced

PIECRUST

2 cups all-purpose flour
¾ teaspoon sea salt

⅔ cup shortening, preferably
non-hydrogenated
6 tablespoons cold water

Preheat the oven to 425°F.

In a saucepan over medium heat, melt the soy butter. Add the flour and stir until the consistency is pasty. Add the water, granulated sugar, brown sugar, and cinnamon. Bring to a gentle boil. Reduce the heat and simmer for 2 minutes. Set aside.

To make the piecrust, in a medium bowl, combine the flour and salt. Using a fork or pastry cutter, cut in the shortening until the mixture is crumbly. Slowly add the water, and toss with a fork until the dough forms a ball. Divide the dough into 2 balls, one slightly larger than the other.

On a floured surface, roll out the larger ball to fit a 9-inch pie pan. Transfer the dough to the pie pan and fill with the peeled and sliced apples. Pour the reserved butter mixture over the apples.

Roll out the second dough ball, cut slits into the dough, and use to cover the top of the pie. Pinch the edges of the dough together. Bake for 15 minutes. Reduce the heat to 350°F and cook for 35 minutes longer, or until the apple filling begins bubbling through the upper piecrust slits.

Yields one 9-inch pie

Justin's 5-Star Truffles

*F*ungi truffles from the ground are often described as "diamonds in the kitchen." And when it comes to rustic-looking chocolate truffles—named after the real thing—they're the diamonds in our shop, eliciting countless "mmms" from our customers all day long. Fortunately, Justin can eat chocolate—dairy-free dark chocolate, that is. Since our shop's House Truffle is laced with heavy cream and butter—pure poison to Justin—we had to experiment like any good food scientist in the kitchen lab. Sous chef Francie helped Ginger create the perfect cocoa-dusted truffle just for Justin. These sinfully mouthwatering nuggets of pleasure, with a hint of cinnamon, rival any in our shop.

When our young food critic tasted his first truffle, he raised five cocoa-covered fingers and exclaimed, "Five-stars!"

Then he high-fived us both.

You can make these truffles with or without a chocolate shell. True, this process is a messy one but a fun, kid-friendly project. Like finger painting!

TRUFFLES

16 ounces dairy-free semi-sweet chocolate chips

⅔ cup soy creamer

6 tablespoons soy butter, at room temperature

1 teaspoon pure vanilla extract

⅓ cup unsweetened cocoa powder

1 teaspoon ground cinnamon

OPTIONAL CHOCOLATE SHELL

2 pounds dairy-free semi-sweet chocolate chips,

for chocolate shell (optional)

In a large glass microwave-safe bowl, combine the chocolate chips and soy creamer. Microwave for 2 minutes, then whisk until smooth. Add the soy butter and vanilla and continue to whisk until velvety. Pour the chocolate mixture, known as a ganache, into a 13 × 9 × 2-inch glass baking dish. Cover with plastic wrap and refrigerate for at least 4 hours.

In the meantime, combine the cocoa and cinnamon in a small bowl and set aside. When the ganache is chilled, using a mini ice cream scoop, form 1-inch balls.

If coating with an optional chocolate shell, freeze the balls for 2 to 3 hours. If not, roll cach ball in the cocoa-cinnamon mixture. The truffles are ready to eat now, or store in the freezer or refrigerator in an airtight container.

To make the optional chocolate shell you need to understand tempering. Tempering chocolate is a process of heating and cooling chocolate for dipping, allowing the crystals in the chocolate to be distributed and suspended evenly throughout the final product to ensure the perfect snap, taste, and beautiful patina to your truffles. If you don't temper the chocolate, bloom will occur: cocoa butter separates from the chocolate, causing it to cast a white film.

Put two-thirds of the chocolate chips into a large microwave-safe glass bowl. Set aside the remaining one-third of the chocolate chips. Place the bowl in the microwave oven on half-power and heat for 1 minute. Remove from the microwave and stir. Repeat this process at least 5 times, or until the chocolate is completely melted, making sure not to burn the chocolate. Remove the bowl from the microwave; the temperature of the chocolate should be approximately 110°F. Stir in the remaining one-third chocolate chips; the temperature of the chocolate should cool down to approximately 85°F.

Now the messy process begins! You can use a fork, but your fingers work better: Hold a frozen ganache ball with two fingers and dip it into the warm bath of chocolate, covering the entire ball. Shake off excess chocolate from your fingers. Place the coated ganache ball onto a wax or parchment paper–lined baking sheet and repeat until all the balls are dipped. Allow your truffles to set for 10 minutes.

For the finishing touch, place half the cocoa and half the cinnamon in a large plastic ziplock bag. Place half of the set truffles into the bag and gently shake until each truffle is coated. Repeat the process to coat the remaining truffles.

Serve your 5-Star Truffles at room temperature, or store in the freezer or refrigerator for future indulgence.

Yields about 45 truffles

ALLERGY REPORT 2011–2012
AGE: THIRTEEN

*D*espite the allergist's recommendation for Justin to undergo RAST blood tests, we waited almost a full year before subjecting him, and frankly us. It's painful to get your hopes up, only to have them dashed. And, of course, imagine the child: Although Justin was a brave kid who rarely complained, we'd be kidding ourselves to think that his spirits went unscathed by being the most allergic child in his class, year after year. It was July, and soon Justin would be entering the eighth grade. No longer our "little guy," he was taller than both of us now and his voice was changing. We hoped for one more change.

Wouldn't it be wonderful to start out the school year on a good food note?

On the day of the appointment to learn the blood test results (the doctor's office wouldn't divulge the results over the phone), Francie was too nervous to go with Ginger and Justin. The image of her nephew drinking milk had been playing like a film in her head every day. But that didn't mean he could drink milk today. Nearly two long hours after the scheduled appointment, she finally got the call from Justin.

"The doctor says I've outgrown my milk and egg allergy!"

Yelling in the background was Ginger, who couldn't contain her excitement. "And his peanut numbers were low, too! The doctor's confident he'll outgrow his peanut allergy someday!"

Apparently, Justin tested negative for milk and egg allergy. But before he could celebrate with a milk shake or an omelet, he would have to undergo a cooked food challenge that could be performed at home with both allergens cooked into muffins and baked at 400 degrees for a minimum of twenty minutes to break down the milk and egg protein, thus reducing the possibility of a severe allergic reaction. If there was no reaction,

Justin would undergo the next test—an in-office raw food challenge.

Ginger, however, just wasn't quite comfortable with conducting the cooked food challenge at home, and insisted it be done in a controlled environment. So be it.

On the day of the "Cooked Milk and Egg Challenge," Francie met Ginger, Justin, and Skip at the allergist's office. All of us were cautiously excited.

Ginger, as instructed by the allergist, had previously made a dozen muffins, containing one cup of milk and two eggs that she had baked at 400 degrees for twenty minutes, and had brought several of these muffins with her. However, we soon learned she was supposed to bake *some* muffins containing milk and *other* muffins containing egg. That way, if Justin had a reaction to a muffin, they could identify which allergen was the culprit. Darn it, the in-office food challenge was cancelled.

"But based on his RAST results," the allergist confidently stated, "you can do the challenge at home."

We left the office a bit deflated by the setback. A

little nervous, too: Conduct the food challenge at home?

Back at home, Ginger went to work in the kitchen, making a batch of muffins with a cup of milk—basically our Round-the-Clock "Milk" Muffins but substituting real milk for the soy milk. The doctor's orders were to initially have Justin eat one-sixth of a muffin and wait twenty minutes. If he had no adverse reaction, Ginger was to give him another portion, until Justin had digested half the muffin. We followed our instructions and. . . .

Success!

The following day, we gave him one-third of a muffin every twenty minutes until the whole muffin was gone.

Success!

The day after that, we began feeding Justin one muffin a day for a week. Then we repeated this at-home food challenge with muffins that also contained two eggs.

Success!

The time had come for another food challenge in a

controlled environment, but this time we were talking a raw food challenge.

We returned to the allergist's office in August toting a bag of shredded cheddar cheese, a carton of milk, and a digital camera—after all, this could be The Big Day! Justin's appointment was for 9:30 A.M. Francie took two pictures of Justin on the examination table waiting for the nurse. We held our breaths, and looked at the clock above the examination table. Tick, tock. The nurse brought in his food sample, just a few shreds of cheddar cheese, on a white plastic spoon. As Justin was taking his first taste of cheese, Francie snapped another picture.

Justin winced. "This tastes weird!"

"Of course it does," Ginger told him. "You've never tasted real cheese before."

He shrugged, unimpressed. "I like my cheese better."

All eyes were on the patient. Momentarily, the allergist joined us. At first Justin seemed fine but in a few minutes he said: "My throat feels a little funny."

The allergist didn't panic. She asked Justin if he felt like his throat was swelling or closing up.

Justin shook his head. "It just felt strange, but it feels fine now," he said.

The allergist indicated that Justin might be reacting because this was the first milk protein to touch his throat since his first birthday. But soon a tiny hive developed on his neck. She explained that the hive could be either allergy- or emotionally induced. After all, there were a lot of nerves going around the room. She asked the nurse to bring Justin some Benadryl.

"To be on the safe side," the allergist said, "why don't you continue your home food challenge, slowly increasing Justin's muffin intake to a few a day with meals and in lieu of other snacks? That will build up his tolerance, and we can retest him in the near future."

"OK," Ginger said as we all exchanged sighs. We'd been hoping for a more celebratory day. Definitive news.

Just then Skip noticed something. By now it was past ten o'clock but the clock read 9:44.

"Doctor, I think your clock stopped."

The allergist looked surprised. "You're right."

Later that day, Francie loaded the pictures onto her laptop. That's when she noticed something unusual: In the picture of Justin waiting for the nurse, the clock on the wall read 9:39. In the picture where he took his first bite of cheese, it read 9:44. But the clock never moved past that minute. In other words, that's when the clock stopped.

We took this as a sign: Perhaps Justin was on his way to outgrowing his allergies—but now wasn't quite the time.

In the summer of 2012, we decided it was time for another raw food challenge in the doctor's office. Justin was a little tentative—anticipating an allergic reaction is never fun and, indeed, nerves alone can cause hives!— but he was ready to give it another try. After all, living an allergy-free life would be a dream come true. However, when we called to make an appointment, the office receptionist informed us that Justin's doctor had just given birth to twins, and was on indefinite maternity leave. Like the clock, maybe this was another sign. Instead of starting the process over with a new doctor, we decided to wait on the raw-food challenge and continue with our home food challenge—cooking eggs and milk into Justin's food in order to build up his tolerance. Was Justin a little disappointed?

"Nah," he replied. "How can I be disappointed when I eat like a king?"

Yes, Justin was happy, and that's all that really mattered.

INDEX

Index

Index

Index

Index

Index